My First Crochet Book

35 fun and easy crochet projects for children aged 7+

CICO **kidz**

Published in 2013 by CICO Kidz
An imprint of Ryland Peters & Small
519 Broadway, 5th Floor, New York
NY 10012
20–21 Jockey's Fields, London
WC1R 4BW
www.cicobooks.com

10 9 8 7 6 5 4 3 2 1

A CIP catalog record for this book is
available from the Library of
Congress and the British Library.

ISBN: 978-1-908862-57-0

Printed in China

Editor: Katie Hardwicke
Consultants: Marie Clayton and
Gillian Tickle
Designer: Elizabeth Healey
Step artworks: Rachel Boulton
Animal artworks: Hannah George
Photographers: Emma Mitchell and
Martin Norris
For further photography credits, see
page 128.

My First Crochet Book

Contents

Introduction

Levels

These are quick, easy projects that use just one or two crochet stitches.

These projects take a little longer and may use some more advanced techniques and some sewing.

These projects may have several stages and require more difficult crochet and sewing techniques. You may need help from an adult.

Crochet is a great craft that you can quickly learn yourself with just a hook and some yarn. You'll soon be able to make hats, bags, cushions and cute toys in funky colours, to keep for yourself or to give as gifts. In this book there are four chapters: Clothes and Accessories, with bags, belts, hats and scarves that will add some fun to your wardrobe; Jewellery, where you'll find a beaded necklace, bracelets, some pretty brooches and even a tiara; Bedroom Essentials, with some fabulous ideas for adding comfy and colourful cushions and storage ideas to liven up your room; and Perfect Gifts, where you'll find things to make that are ideal presents for your family and all your friends.

Crochet is a great hobby for when you have a quiet moment, perhaps on a long journey, on holiday or on a rainy afternoon. Why not invite a friend over to crochet with you, too? Crochet can be a bit fiddly to learn at the start, but you'll soon master the basic stitches. You can start by learning to make chains, and turn these into friendship bracelets to share. And once you learn to crochet in the round you'll be amazed at how quickly you can create something really impressive, like the cute Mushroom on page 116, or the groovy Round Stripy Cushion Cover on page 93.

To help you decide what to make, we have marked all the projects with one, two or three smiley faces to show how easy or difficult they are. Projects marked with one smiley face are the easiest, two smiley faces mean the project is slightly harder, and those with three smiley faces are the ones to tackle once you've had a bit of practise.

There's a list of all the crochet stitches and techniques you will use at the start of each project, and the pages where you can find the stitch and technique instructions if you need them. There is also a list of everything you will need for each project, including the yarns and colours used in the projects. If you want to, you can choose your own colours and even a different brand of yarn – as long as you use a similar type of yarn (such as double knitting or Aran) and the same size hook, the pattern will still work. Some projects need buttons, felt, and scraps of fabric or ribbons, so it's good to put together a sewing box that contains the basics – then you'll be ready to create anything!

Tools and materials

You need just two items to start crocheting: a hook and some yarn. However, there are a few other bits and pieces that you'll need to make some of the projects in this book — but none of them are expensive and you'll probably have some of them at home already.

Crochet hook

Hooks come in different materials and sizes. Each pattern tells you the size you'll need to make the project.

Beads

These are great for adding extra decoration or sparkle to a project. Just sew them on when the crochet is complete or crochet them into the pattern.

Stitch marker

Markers are used, especially in rounds, where you need to keep track of the beginning of a row or a certain point in your crochet. You can use a piece of thread in a bright colour or a shop-bought marker that looks like a safety pin.

Buttons

Another way of adding colour and decoration, buttons are especially good as eyes for toys.

Scissors

Always cut your yarn with scissors, don't break it, even when the pattern says 'break yarn'.

Sewing needle and thread

You'll need these to sew decorations and felt additions to your projects.

Scraps of fabric

Keep a sewing basket with scraps of fabric, felt, ribbons and trimmings close by you to help finish some of the projects and add your own personal touch.

Yarns

You can crochet with all the same yarns that are used for knitting, including some metallic yarns and even string or twine. The projects give you the brand and type of yarn used but if you can't find an exact match you will still be able to crochet using a similar type of yarn. For example, if the pattern uses an Aran weight yarn, any type of Aran yarn can be substituted.

You can find details of the type of yarn on the ball label, together with suggestions for hook sizes.

Crochet techniques

Getting started

Holding the hook

There are two ways of holding the hook in crochet, and you can choose whichever of these feels most natural for you.

Holding the hook like a pen

Holding the hook like a knife

1 Pick up your hook in your right hand if you are right-handed, or left if you are left-handed, as though you were picking up a pen or pencil, or as if you were picking up a knife, if that feels more comfortable.

2 Keeping the hook held loosely between your fingers and thumb, turn your hand so that the palm is facing up and the hook is balanced in your hand and resting in the space between your index finger and your thumb.

Slip knot

The first loop on the hook in crochet is created by a slip knot.

1 Make a loop of the yarn around your fingers, so that the loop is facing downwards. Hold the loop at the top, where the yarn crosses, and let the tail drop down so that it falls in the centre of the loop. With your free hand or the tip of a crochet hook, pull the tail through the loop so that it makes a second loop (do not pull the end of the yarn all the way through). Pull the knot, so that it tightens loosely.

2 Slip the hook into the second loop and pull the loop taut around the hook. Do not pull it too tightly or the first chain will be hard to make.

Holding the yarn

(1) Pick up the yarn from the ball with your little finger of the opposite hand to your hook, with your palm facing upwards – so if you are right-handed pick it up with your left hand, if you are left-handed, pick it up with your right hand.

(2) Turn your hand to face downwards, with the yarn on top of your index finger and under the other two fingers and wrapped right around the little finger. Hold the hook steady just under the slip knot, then use your left index finger to create tension in the yarn by keeping it held above the work.

Crochet stitches

Yarn round hook

To create a stitch, you'll need to catch the yarn with the hook and pull it through the loop.

(1) Holding the yarn and hook in the appropriate hands, hold the tail end of the yarn under the slip knot and catch the working yarn (the ball end) from behind with the hook pointed upwards.

(2) As you gently pull the yarn through the loop on the hook, turn the hook so that it faces downwards and slide the yarn through the loop. The loop on the hook should be kept loose enough so that the hook slides through easily.

Chain

Most crochet projects begin with a length of chain. This is the perfect stitch to practise your tension on, as it is the simplest thing you can do in crochet.

(1) Using the hook, wrap the yarn round the hook (see above) and pull it through the loop on the hook, creating a new loop on the hook. One chain is made.

(2) Making sure the stitches are even – not too loose or tight – repeat step 1 to make a length of chain. Keep moving your middle finger and thumb close to the tip of the hook, to hold the work in place with the opposite hand that you hold your hook with.

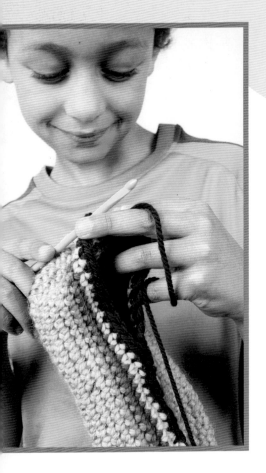

Slip stitch

A slip stitch doesn't create any height and is often used as the last stitch to create a smooth and even round or row.

1 To make a slip stitch, put the hook through the work, yarn round hook.

2 Pull the yarn through both the work and through the loop on the hook at the same time. One slip stitch made.

Double crochet (dc)

This is the next crochet stitch to learn once you have got chain right.

1 Make one chain (see page 11). This is called the 'turning chain' and you make one at the start of every row of double crochet. Missing the chain you have just made, insert the hook from front to back into the next stitch.

2 There should be the two strands of the stitch and one loop on the hook. Yarn round hook and pull the yarn through the work to the front. Yarn round hook again.

3 Yarn round hook again and pull the yarn through the two loops on the hook. You will then have one loop on the hook. One double crochet made.

Half treble (htr)

This stitch involves a third loop on the hook. You need to work two chain (see page 11) for the turning chain at the start of a row of half treble crochet.

1 Yarn round hook before you insert the hook. Insert the hook in the next stitch, from front to back .

2 Yarn round hook again and pull through the first loop on the hook only (you now have three loops on the hook).

3 Yarn round hook and pull the yarn through all three loops. You'll be left with one loop on the hook. One half-treble made.

Treble (tr)

1 Work three chain (see page 11) for the turning chain at the start of a row of treble crochet. Before inserting the hook into the work, wrap the yarn round the hook and insert the hook through the work with the yarn wrapped around.

2 Yarn round hook again and pull through the first loop on the hook (you now have three loops on the hook). Yarn round hook again, pull the yarn through two loops (you now have two loops on the hook).

3 Yarn round hook and pull the yarn through the two loops. You will be left with one loop on the hook. One treble made.

Double treble (dtr)

1 Work four chain for the turning chain. Take the yarn round the hook twice, insert the hook into the fifth chain from the hook, yarn round hook, pull a loop through (you now have four loops on the hook). Yarn round hook, pull the yarn through the first two stitches on the hook.

2 There are now three loops on hook. Yarn round hook again, pull a loop through the next two stitches.

3 There are now two loops on hook. Yarn round hook, pull a loop through the last two stitches. You will be left with one loop on the hook. One double treble made.

Triple treble (trtr)

Work five chain for the turning chain. Yarn round hook three times, insert hook into the stitch, yarn round hook, pull a loop through (five loops on hook), yarn round hook, pull the yarn through two stitches (four loops on hook), yarn round hook, pull a loop through the next two stitches (three loops on hook), yarn round hook, pull a loop through the next two stitches (two loops on hook), yarn round hook, pull a loop through the last two stitches. One triple treble made.

Increasing

To work an extra stitch, you simply need to work into the same stitch more than once. Make two or three stitches into one stitch from the previous row.

The illustration shows a two-stitch increase being made.

Decreasing

You can decrease by either missing the next stitch and continuing to crochet, or by crocheting two or more stitches together.

Double crochet two stitches together (dc2tog)

1 Insert the hook into the next stitch, yarn round hook, draw a loop through the stitch, but do not finish the double crochet stitch as usual.

2 Insert the hook in to the next stitch, yarn round hook. Draw the loop through the stitch only (there should be three loops on the hook). Yarn round hook and pull through all three loops on the hook.

Half treble two stitches together (htr2tog)

Yarn round hook, insert hook into next st, yarn round hook, draw a loop through, insert hook into next st, draw a loop through, yarn round hook and pull through all four loops.

Starting to work in the round

If you are crocheting a round shape, one way of starting off is by crocheting a number of chains following the instructions in your pattern, and then joining them into a ring.

1 Work a chain to the length given in the pattern. To join the chain into a circle, insert the crochet hook into the first chain that you made (not into the slip knot) – this creates a horseshoe shape. Yarn round hook, then pull the yarn through the chain and through the loop on your hook at the same time, creating a slip stitch and forming a ring.

2 You now have a ring. You can either work a continuous spiral (without making a turning chain at the start or joining with a slip stitch at the end), or in complete rounds (see Making fabric on page 16).

Marking rounds with a stitch marker

When rounds are worked in a spiral you do not need to make chain at the start or join the end with a slip stitch, but you will need to know where the round begins and ends.

1 To help you keep your place, mark the beginning of the round with a stitch marker – a piece of yarn in a contrasting colour is useful for this or use a shop-bought marker. Loop the stitch marker into the first stitch.

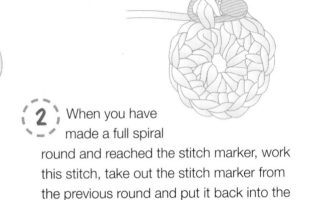

2 When you have made a full spiral round and reached the stitch marker, work this stitch, take out the stitch marker from the previous round and put it back into the first stitch of the new round.

Other useful techniques

Turn

This is used when working in rows. Keep the last loop on your crochet hook and turn your work towards you so that it is positioned under your yarn hand. You can then work back down the row on the opposite side.

Making fabric

When making rows or complete rounds you need to make a turning chain at the start or end of the row or round to create the height you need for the stitch you are working. The number of chain needed for each stitch is as follows:

Double crochet – 1 chain
Half treble crochet - 2 chain
Treble crochet – 3 chain
Double treble crochet – 4 chain
Triple treble crochet – 5 chain

Working straight

Work 1 round or row straight means to work the next round without increasing or decreasing any stitches.

Working into back loop (blo)

Insert the hook into the back loop of the next stitch only.

Working into front loop (tfl)

Insert the hook into the front of the next stitch only.

Working into a chain space

Insert the hook into the space between stitches in the row below instead of into the top of the stitch.

Fastening off

When you have finished crocheting, you need to fasten off the stitches to stop all your work unravelling.

Pull up the final loop of the last stitch to make it bigger. Cut the yarn, leaving a tail of approx 10cm (4in). Pull the tail all the way through the loop and pull the loop up tightly.

Joining in new yarn

Sometimes you will need to change yarn colour, but it's very easy to do.

1 Fasten off the old colour (see above). Make a slip knot with the new colour (see page 10). Insert the hook into the stitch at the beginning of the next row, then insert the hook through the slip knot.

2 Pull the loop of the slip knot through to the front of the work. Yarn round hook with the new colour. Work one chain (see page 11) to hold the new colour in place, then complete the first stitch as normal.

Weaving in yarn ends

It is important to finish your crochet correctly and weave in the tail ends of the yarn so that they are secure and your crochet won't unravel. Thread a darning needle with the tail end of yarn. On the wrong side, take the needle through the crochet one stitch down on the edge, then take it through the stitches, working in a gentle zigzag. Work through 4 or 5 stitches then return in the opposite direction. Remove the needle, pull the crochet gently to stretch it, and trim the end.

Sewing up

Sewing up crochet fabric can be done in many ways, but using a whip stitch is the easiest. However, you will be able to see the stitches clearly so you can make a feature of them by using a different colour yarn to the one used in the project.

Lay the two pieces to be joined next to each other with right sides facing upwards. Secure the yarn to one piece. Insert the needle into the front of one piece of fabric, then up from the back of the adjoining fabric. Repeat along the seam.

Sewing on buttons

You can use buttons as decorations — and you never know when you'll need to sew a button onto a piece of clothing!

1 Mark the place where you want the button to go. Push the needle up from the back of the fabric and sew a few stitches round and round in this place.

2 Now bring the needle up through one of the holes in the button. Push the needle back down through the second hole and through the fabric. Bring it back up through the first hole. Repeat this five or six times. If there are four holes in the button, use all four of them to make a cross pattern. Make sure that you keep the stitches close together under the middle of the button.

3 Finish with a few small stitches round and round on the back of the fabric and then trim the thread.

Following crochet patterns

To make the projects in this book, you will need to follow the patterns. These give instructions on how many and what type of stitches you need. Crochet patterns use abbreviations for the stitches, such as ch for chain and dc for double crochet. Patterns combine different numbers of stitches and, sometimes, different types of stitches, to make the shape of the crocheted piece.

Crochet patterns are written out as instructions, one row or round at a time. Start by making the number of chains required and then work each row. To help you to keep track of where you are, tick off each row with a pencil when you have completed it.

Sometimes the pattern will include the number of stitches that you should have at the end of each row, shown in brackets. Check that your stitch number matches.

First, practise the basic stitches, how to join in new colours and fasten off, by making a few rectangles or circles. Once you feel happy that you can work all the different types of stitches, you will be ready to start on your very own project.

Finishing your project will involve some different techniques, from sewing up the pieces to sewing on buttons or attaching pompoms. You'll find instructions on how to do this with each project.

Abbreviations

The following abbreviations are used in the crochet patterns.

beg beginning

blo back loop only

ch chain

ch sp chain space

cont continue

cm centimetres

dc double crochet

dc2tog double crochet 2 together

htr half treble

dtr double treble

htr2tog half treble 2 together

in inches

rem remain(ing)

rep repeat

rnd round

sl st slip stitch

st(s) stitch(es)

sp space

tfl through front loop

tr treble

trtr triple treble

CHAPTER 1

Clothes and Accessories

Belt

An extremely simple belt, which can easily be made longer or shorter or wider, as you wish.

You will need

1 x 50g ball (125m/137yd) Debbie Bliss Ecobaby (100% organic cotton), in each of:

Yarn A: shade 04, aqua

Yarn B: shade 14, lemon

Yarn C: shade 23, peach

Yarn D: shade 24, salmon

3.25mm crochet hook

Two very small buttons, approx 1cm (½in) diameter

Sewing needle and thread

Measurements

One size, 2.5cm (1in) wide and 92cm (36in) long

Tension

Approx 20 sts and 13.5 rows to 10cm (4in) in htr using 3.25mm hook, or size required to obtain correct tension.

1 Crochet the belt

Using 3.25mm hook and yarn A, ch172.
Row 1: 1htr in 2nd ch from hook, 1htr in each ch to end of row, turn. (170 htr)
Change to yarn B, fasten off yarn A, and work 1 row straight in htr, turn.
Change to yarn C, fasten off yarn B, and work 1 row straight in htr, turn.
Change to yarn D, fasten off yarn C, and work 1 row straight in htr.
Fasten off yarn.

2 Finish the belt

Weave in the loose ends with a darning needle.

3 Attach the buttons

Sew the buttons to one end of the belt. To fasten around your waist, insert the buttons through holes between stitches at the place where the belt fits you.

Perfect with any outfit!

Abbreviations (see page 19)

ch chain
htr half treble crochet

Techniques (see pages 10–19)

Fastening off

Joining in a new colour

Turn

Sewing on buttons

Cowl

A very quick project, worked in the round, so no sewing up! Try using lots of different scraps of yarn for a rainbow-coloured neck warmer.

You will need

1 x 100g ball (132m/144yd) Artesano Aran (50% superfine alpaca, 50% Peruvian highland wool), in each of:

Yarn A: shade 2184, meadle

Yarn B: shade 5083, lomond

5mm crochet hook

Darning needle

Measurements

One size, approx 10cm (4in) wide and 120cm (47in) around

Tension

Approx 3 grouped treble crochets and 7 rows to 10cm (4in) using 5mm hook, or size required to obtain correct tension.

1 Crochet the cowl

Using 5mm hook and yarn A, ch120, join into a ring with a sl st into first ch, trying not to twist the chain.

Rnd 1: Ch3, 2tr into bottom of same ch, ch1, miss 2 ch, *3tr in next ch, ch1, miss 2 ch; rep from * to end of rnd, join to top of 3-ch with a sl st.

Rnd 2: Sl st in next 1-ch sp, ch3, 2tr in 1-ch sp, ch1, *3tr in next 1-ch sp, ch1; rep from * to end of rnd, join to top of 3-ch with a sl st. Fasten off yarn A.

Rnd 3: Join yarn B to any 1-ch sp with a sl st, ch3, 2tr in 1-ch sp, ch1, *3tr in next 1-ch sp, ch1; rep from * to end of rnd, join to top of 3-ch with a sl st.
Fasten off yarn B.

Rnd 4: Join yarn A to any 1-ch sp with a sl st, ch3, 2tr in 1-ch sp, ch1, *3tr in next 1-ch sp, ch1; rep from * to end of rnd, join to top of 3-ch with a sl st.
Fasten off yarn A.

Rnd 5: Rep Rnd 3.
Fasten off yarn B.

Rnd 6: Join yarn A to any 1-ch sp with a sl st, ch3, 2tr in 1-ch sp, ch1, *3tr in next 1-ch sp, ch1; rep from * to end of rnd, join to top of 3-ch with a sl st.

Rnd 7: Sl st to next 1-ch sp, ch3, 2tr in 1-ch sp, ch1, *3tr in next 1-ch sp, ch1; rep from * to end of rnd, join to top of 3-ch with a sl st.
Fasten off yarn.

2 Finish the cowl

Use the darning needle to weave in the ends of the yarn.

Abbreviations (see page 19)

ch chain

ch sp chain space

rep repeat

rnd round

sl st slip stitch

sp space

tr treble crochet

Techniques (see pages 10–19)

Fastening off

Joining in a new colour

Making fabric

Starting to work in the round

NOTE The cowl is worked in complete rounds.

3 Blocking

Ask an adult to help you carefully press the cowl into shape on a soft surface. Use a medium hot iron and put a clean cloth or tea towel over the crochet to protect it from the iron. This is known as blocking.

Flower earmuffs

If you don't like hats, but can't stand having cold ears, earmuffs are for you — and they are also great for when your friends just talk too loudly!

You will need

1 x 50g ball (120m/131yd) Rico Essentials Merino DK (100% merino wool), in each of:

Yarn A: shade 19, mulberry

Yarn B: shade 01, rose

Yarn C: shade 04, acacia

4mm crochet hook

Stitch marker

Darning needle

Toy stuffing

Measurements

One size, approx 29cm (11½in) from centre of one earmuff, across strap, to centre of other earmuff

Tension

Approx 22 sts and 20 rows to 10cm (4in) in dc using 4mm crochet hook, or size required to obtain correct tension.

(1) Crochet the strap

Using 4mm crochet hook and yarn A, ch13.

Row 1: 1dc in 2nd ch from hook, 1dc in each ch to end of row, turn. (12 dc)

Row 2: Ch1, dc in each st across row, turn.

Rep last row until strap is approx 28cm (11in) long.

Fasten off yarn.

(2) Crochet the earpieces (make 4)

Using 4mm crochet hook and yarn A, ch2.

Rnd 1: 6dc in first ch made, do not join rnd.

Rnd 2: 2dc in each dc around. (12 dc)

Rnd 3: [2dc in next st, 1dc] around. (18 dc)

Rnd 4: [2dc in next st, 2dc] around. (24 dc)

Rnd 5: [2dc in next st, 3dc] around. (30 dc)

Rnd 6: [2dc in next st, 4dc] around. (36 dc)

Rnd 7: [2dc in next st, 5dc] around. (42 dc)

Rnd 8: [2dc in next st, 6dc] around. (48 dc)

Rnd 9: [2dc in next st, 7dc] around. (54 dc)

Rnd 10: [2dc in next st, 8dc] around. (60 dc)

Fasten off yarn.

For a matching skinny scarf, simply follow the pattern for the strap and make it longer.

Abbreviations (see page 19)

ch chain

dc double crochet

dc2tog double crochet 2 together

rep repeat

rnd round

sl st slip stitch

Techniques (see pages 10–19)

Fastening off

Joining in a new colour

Marking rounds with a stitch marker

Sewing up

Starting to work in the round

Turn

NOTE Earpieces are worked in continuous spiral rounds, do not turn throughout and do not join rounds.

Flowers are worked in complete rounds, joining each round with a sl st.

The strap is worked in rows, turn at the end of each row.

3 Crochet the flowers

Using 4mm crochet hook and yarn A, ch6 and join into a ring with a sl st into first ch.

Rnd 1: Ch1, 12dc into ring, join with a sl st into top of 1-ch. Fasten off yarn A and join in yarn B to any dc.

Rnd 2: 1dc in same st as join [ch5, miss 1dc, 1dc in next st] six times, finishing last rep with a sl st in next st. (6 petals)

Rnd 3: [9dc in next ch sp, sl st in dc] around. Fasten off yarn B and join yarn A to any dc, work 1 rnd in dc all around petal edges. Fasten off yarn.

4 Crochet the ties

Using 4mm crochet hook and yarns B and C held together, crochet two lengths of chain, each approx 50cm (20in) long. When working with two strands, treat them as one, hooking and pulling them through the loops together.

5 Sew the earpieces

Weave in all the loose ends with the darning needle. Take two of the circles that you made for the earpieces and sew them together around the edge, leaving a gap in the edge to stuff them. Fill the earpiece with toy stuffing until it is firm and well-rounded, and then sew up the gap. Repeat with the remaining two circles.

6 Sew on the flowers

Sew a flower to the top of each earpiece, taking a few stitches through the middle with matching yarn. Sew the earpieces to the ends of the strap, with the flowers facing out.

Wrap up warm!

7 Add the ties

Sew one chain to the bottom of each earpiece to make the ties and finish the earmuffs.

Floral purse

This is a really pretty purse to make and a great beginner's project, which takes only a small amount of time to achieve maximum effect.

You will need

1 x 50g ball (90m/98yd) Debbie Bliss Cashmerino Aran (55% merino wool, 33% microfibre, 12% cashmere) in:

Yarn A: shade 011, green

Small lengths of DK yarn in pinks, purples, blues and yellow for flowers

4.5mm and 4mm crochet hooks

Darning needle

1 button, 1cm (½in) diameter

Sewing needle and thread

Measurements

Approx 15 x 10cm (6 x 4in)

Tension

Exact tension isn't important for this project.

1 Crochet the purse

Using 4.5mm hook and yarn A, ch24.

Row 1: 1htr in second ch from hook, 1htr in each ch to end, 2ch, turn. (22 sts – 2ch counts as first htr).

Row 2: 1htr in each st, 2ch, turn.

Rep Row 2 until work measures approx 19cm (7½in).

2 Crochet the flap

Rows 1–4: Ch2, htr2tog, 1htr in each st to end, turn. (18 sts)

Rows 5–7: Ch2, htr2tog, 1htr in each st to last 2 sts, htr2tog, turn. (12 sts)

3 Make a buttonhole

Row 1: Ch2, htr2tog, 1htr in each of next 2 sts, 2ch, miss 2 sts, 1htr in each of next 3 sts, htr2tog, turn.

Row 2: Ch2, htr2tog, 1htr in next st, 2htr in ch sp, 1htr in each of next 3 sts, turn. (8 sts)

Pretty flowers for a special purse

4 **Crochet the edging**
Turn and make 32dc sts along first side, 3dc into corner st, 22dc sts along bottom edge, 3dc into corner st, 32dc sts along second side.
Fasten off yarn.

Abbreviations (see page 19)

ch chain

ch sp chain space

dc double crochet

htr half treble

htr2tog half treble 2 together

rep repeat

rnd round

sl st slip stitch

st(s) stitch(es)

tr treble

Techniques (see pages 10–19)

Fastening off

Joining in a new colour

Turn

Sewing on buttons

Sewing up

Starting to work in the round

5 Crochet the flowers (make 4)

Use two colours for each flower.

Using first colour and 4mm hook, ch6, join into a ring with a sl st into first ch. Make 16dc into ring, joining tail around into each st, join with a sl st.

Fasten off yarn.

Join second colour into fastened-off st.

*Ch3, 1tr in each of next two sts, ch3, sl st in next st; rep from * 4 more times.
(5 petals)

Fasten off yarn.

Pull the yarn tail to close up centre hole and sew in the ends.

6 Sew the purse

Ask an adult to help you block the purse by pressing it lightly with a warm iron, use a tea towel to protect the yarn if necessary. With the wrong side of the purse facing you, turn up the bottom edge to the start of the flap. Using a darning needle and matching yarn, sew the side seams together with whip stitch, leaving the flap open.

7 Finish the purse

Position the button on the front of the purse to correspond with the buttonhole and sew it in place with a sewing needle. Sew three flowers to the front flap and one to the back of the purse.

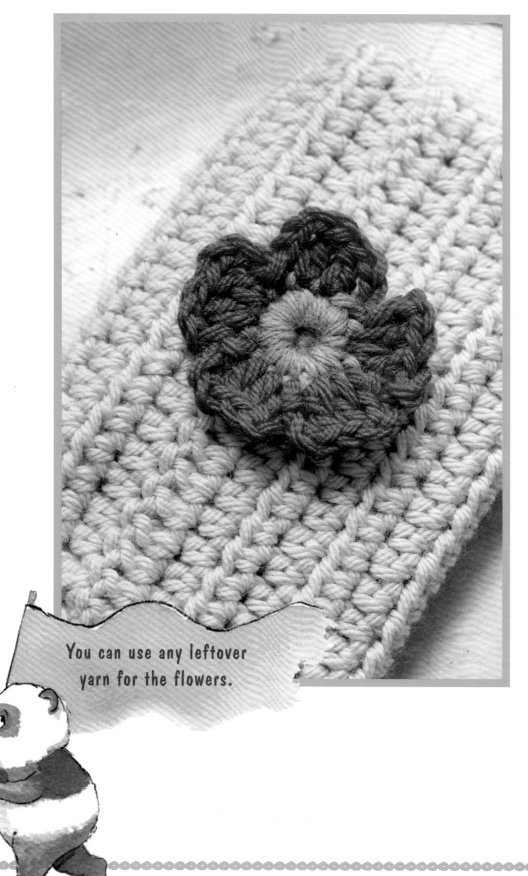

You can use any leftover yarn for the flowers.

Legwarmers

Crochet these cosy legwarmers in one shade or in candy colour stripes. They look great with ballet flats or with ankle boots.

You will need

1 x 50g ball (100m/109yd) Rico Essentials Soft Merino Aran (100% merino wool), in each of:

Yarn A: shade 041, eucalyptus

Yarn B: shade 015, fuchsia

Yarn C: shade 050, pistachio

4.5mm and 5mm crochet hooks

Darning needle

Measurements

One size, approx 26cm (10¼in) long and 14cm (5½in) wide, but you can make them longer or shorter by working more or fewer rounds

Tension

Approx 11 sts and 10 rows to 10cm (4in) in pattern using 5mm hook, or size required to obtain correct tension.

1 Crochet the legwarmers (make 2)

Using 4.5mm hook and yarn A, ch34, join into a ring with a sl st into first ch.

Rnd 1: Ch2, miss next ch, [1dc in next ch, ch1, miss next ch] to end, join with a sl st into top of 2-ch.

Rnd 2: Ch1, 1dc in 1-ch sp, [ch1, 1dc in 1-ch sp] to end, join with a sl st into top of first 1-ch.

Rnd 3: Ch2, [1dc in next 1-ch sp, ch1] to end, join with a sl st into top of 2-ch.

Change to yarn B and larger 5mm hook.

Rnd 4: Ch3, 1tr in each dc and 1-ch sp around, join with a sl st into top of 3-ch. (34 sts)

Change to yarn C and work two rnds straight in tr.

**Change to yarn A and work one rnd straight in dc.

Change to yarn B and work one rnd straight in tr.

Change to yarn C and work two rnds straight in tr.**

Rep from ** to ** three times more, or until desired length of legwarmer has been reached.

Change to yarn A and smaller 4.5mm hook.

Next rnd: Ch2, miss next tr [1dc in next tr, ch1, miss next tr] to end, join with a sl st into top of 2-ch.

Next rnd: Ch1, 1dc in 1-ch sp, [ch1, 1dc in 1-ch sp] to end, join with a sl st into top of first 1-ch.

Next rnd: Ch2, [1dc in next 1-ch sp, ch1] to end, join with a sl st into top of 2-ch.

Fasten off yarn.

Keep your ankles cosy

2 Finishing

Use a darning needle to weave in the ends of the different colour yarns.

Abbreviations (see page 19)

ch chain

dc double crochet

rep repeat

rnd round

sl st slip stitch

sp space

st(s) stitch(es)

tr treble crochet

Techniques (see pages 10–19)

Fastening off

Joining in a new colour

Starting to work in the round

Beanie hat

A very cute and simple beanie hat, which will work up in no time at all in the easiest of stitches. You can make it more fun by adding funny animal ears and a face, or just wear it plain and simple!

You will need

1 x 100g ball (200m/218yd) Rico Essentials Soft Merino Aran (100% merino superwash), in each of:

Yarn A: shade 81, fawn

Yarn B: shade 15, violet (only very small quantities used)

4.5mm crochet hook

Darning needle

Scraps of white and coloured felt for the eyes

Sewing needle and thread

Two buttons for eyes

Leftover pink yarn for nose

Measurements

S(M:L)

Finished hat approx 48(52.5:57)cm [19(21:22½)in] unstretched

Tension

17 sts and 21 rows to 10cm (4in) in dc in the round using a 4.5mm hook, or size required to obtain correct tension.

1 Crochet the hat

Using 4.5mm hook and yarn A, ch2.

Rnd 1: 6dc in first ch, join into a ring with a sl st.

Rnd 2: Ch1, 2dc in each st, join with a sl st into top of 1-ch. (12 dc)

Rnd 3: Ch1, [1dc, 2dc in next st] around, join with sl st into top of 1-ch. (18 dc)

Rnd 4: Ch1, [2dc, 2dc in next st] around, join with a sl st into top of 1-ch. (24 dc)

Rnd 5: Ch1, [3dc, 2dc in next st] around, join with a sl st into top of 1-ch. (30 dc)

Rnd 6: Ch1, [4dc, 2dc in next st] around, join with a sl st into top of 1-ch. (36 dc)

Rnd 7: Ch1, [5dc, 2dc in next st] around, join with a sl st into top of 1-ch. (42 dc)

Rnd 8: Ch1, [6dc, 2dc in next st] around, join with a sl st into top of 1-ch. (48 dc)

Rnd 9: Ch1, [7dc, 2dc in next st] around, join with a sl st into top of 1-ch. (54 dc)

Rnd 10: Ch1, [8dc, 2dc in next st] around, join with a sl st into top of 1-ch. (60 dc)

Work 1 rnd straight.

Rnd 12: Ch1, [9dc, 2dc in next st] around, join with a sl st into top of 1-ch. (66 dc)

Work 1 rnd straight.

Rnd 14: Ch1, [10dc, 2dc in next st] around, join with a sl st into top of 1-ch. (72 dc)

Work 1 rnd straight.

Rnd 16: Ch1, [11dc, 2dc in next st] around, join with a sl st into top of 1-ch. (78 dc)

M and L sizes only

Work 1 rnd straight.

Rnd 18: Ch1, [12dc, 2dc in next st] around, join with a sl st into top of 1-ch. (84 dc)

Work 1 rnd straight.

Rnd 20: Ch1, [13dc, 2dc in next st] around, join with a sl st into top of 1-ch. (90 dc)

L size only

Work 1 rnd straight.

Rnd 22: Ch1, [14dc, 2dc in next st] around, join with a sl st into top of 1-ch. (96 dc)

All sizes

Work straight in dc for a further 12(13:14)cm [4¾(5:5½)in].
Fasten off yarn.

Abbreviations (see page 19)

ch chain

dc double crochet

dc2tog double crochet 2 together

rep repeat

rnd round

sl st slip stitch

st(s) stitch(es)

Techniques (see pages 10–19)

Fastening off

Making fabric

Sewing on buttons

Starting to work in the round

Turn

NOTE The beanie is worked in complete rounds.

The ears are worked in rows, turn at the end of each row.

Try making the beanie in black and white for a very stylish panda version!

2. Crochet the ears (make 2)

Using 4.5mm hook and yarn A, ch2.
Row 1: 4dc in first ch, turn.
Row 2: Ch1, 2dc in each st to end, turn. (8 dc)
Row 3: Ch1, [1dc, 2dc in next st] to end, turn. (12 dc)
Row 4: Ch1, [2dc, 2dc in next st] to end, turn. (16 dc)
Row 5: Ch1, [3dc, 2dc in next st] to end, turn. (20 dc)
Row 6: Ch1, [4dc, 2dc in next st] to end. (24 dc)
Fasten off yarn.

Using 4.5mm hook and yarn B, ch2.
Row 1: 4dc in first ch, turn.
Row 2: Ch1, 2dc in each st to end, turn. (8 dc)
Row 3: Ch1, [1dc, 2dc in next st] to end, turn. (12 dc)
Row 4: Ch1, [2dc, 2dc in next st] to end, turn. (16 dc)
Row 5: Ch1, [3dc, 2dc in next st] to end. (20 dc)
Fasten off yarn.

3. Sew the ears

Sew the smaller ear piece onto the larger ear piece. Fold the ear along the straight seam, sew the fold together and then sew the ear to the side of the hat.

4. Sew the eyes

Cut two circles from the white felt and two slightly smaller circles from the coloured felt. You can either cut the circles freehand or use something round, such as a large button or cotton reel, to draw around. Sew the white circles to the front of the hat with a sewing needle and thread. Attach the coloured circles over the white circles by sewing the buttons on over them.

Add the nose

5 Using a scrap of yarn, embroider a triangular nose with a few straight stitches that decrease in size.

Make one for your best friend

Squares scarf

Granny squares are traditional, fun and easy to make, and once you start on them, you will quickly become hooked! Join lots of squares together to make a lovely, simple scarf.

You will need

....

1 x 50g ball (90m/98yd) Patons Fairytale Dreamtime DK (100% pure wool), in each of:

Yarn A: shade 4953, pink

Yarn B: shade 4954, lilac

Yarn C: shade 4957, turquoise

Yarn D: shade 4952, lime

Yarn E: shade 4960, yellow

4.5mm crochet hook

Darning needle

Measurements

....

One size, approx 15 x 112cm (6 x 44in)

Tension

....

Each square measures approx 8 x 8cm (3¼ x 3¼in) using a 4.5mm hook, or size required to obtain correct tension.

1 Crochet a square

You can make as many squares as you need, our scarf uses 28. Make an even number if your scarf is going to be 2 squares wide, like ours.

Using any yarn and 4.5mm hook, ch4, join to first ch with a sl st to form ring.

Rnd 1: Ch3 (counts as first tr), 2tr in ring, ch3, [3tr in ring, ch3] three times, join with a sl st to top of first ch, sl st to next 3-ch sp.

Rnd 2: Ch3 (counts as first tr), [2tr, ch3, 3tr] all in same 3-ch sp, ch1, *[3tr, ch3, 3tr] all in next 3-ch sp, ch 1; rep from * twice more, join with a sl st to top of first ch, sl st to next 3-ch sp.

Rnd 3: Ch3 (counts as first tr), [2tr, ch3, 3tr] all in same sp for corner, ch1, 3tr in next 1-ch sp, ch1, *[3tr, ch3, 3tr] all in next 3-ch sp for corner, ch1, 3tr in next 1-ch sp, ch1; rep from * around, join with a sl st to top of first ch, sl st to next 3-ch sp.

Fasten off yarn.

2 Sew the squares together

Lay your finished squares out in the scarf shape, two squares wide. Move the squares around until you are happy with their positions, if you are using different colours. Using a darning needle and matching yarns, sew all the squares together with whip stitch to make a scarf two squares wide and 14 squares long.

Granny will love your granny squares!

Abbreviations (see page 19)

ch chain

ch sp chain space

rep repeat

rnd round

sl st slip stitch

sp space

tr treble crochet

Techniques (see pages 10–19)

Fastening off

Making fabric

Sewing up

Starting to work in the round

Bird bag

A sweet and simple book bag, you can easily make yours into any creature that you wish — ours is a robin redbreast. Try stripes for a tiger!

You will need

1 x 100g ball (132m/144yd) Artesano Aran (50% superfine alpaca, 50% Peruvian highland wool), in each of:

Yarn A: shade 0042, wester

Yarn B: shade 969, ash

5mm crochet hook

Darning needle

Felt and buttons for features

Sewing needle and thread

Measurements

One size, approx 24 x 25cm (9½ x 9¾in)

Tension

Approx 14 htr and 12 rows to 10cm (4in) in htr using 5mm hook, or size required to obtain correct tension.

1 Crochet the bag

Using 5mm hook and yarn A, ch72.

Row 1: 1htr in 3rd ch from hook, 1htr in each ch to end of row, turn. (70 htr)

Row 2: Ch2, 1htr in each st across row, turn.

Work straight in htr as row 2, until work measures approx 18cm (7in).

Change to yarn B and work a further 6cm (2½in) straight in htr.

Fasten off yarn.

2 Crochet the straps (make 2)

Using 5mm hook and yarn A, ch8.

Row 1: 1htr in 3rd ch from hook, 1htr in each ch to end of row, turn. (6 htr)

Row 2: Ch2, htr in each st across row, turn.

Work straight in htr as Row 2, until work measures approx 50cm (20in).

Fasten off yarn.

3 Sew the bag

With the right side facing you, fold the fabric in half widthways (so that the right sides are now together) and stitch the open side and bottom seams together. Turn the bag right side out.

4 Make the eyes and beak

Cut out circles from the pieces of felt – you could draw around something to help you if you're not sure about cutting a circle freehand. Cut off the corner of a piece of felt to make a triangle for the beak.

Abbreviations (see page 19)

ch chain

htr half treble crochet

st(s) stitch(es)

Techniques (see pages 10–19)

Fastening off

Joining in a new colour

Making fabric

Sewing on buttons

Sewing up

Turn

5 Add buttons

Sew the white felt circles for the eyes and the beak to the front of the bag using small overstitches and sewing thread. Attach the green circles to the eyes by sewing them in place with buttons.

6 Attach the straps

Using grey yarn and a darning needle, sew a strap to the top inner edge of each side of the bag, attaching it each end 6cm (2½in) in from the sides. Make sure that the strap isn't twisted before you sew it in place.

Hat with earflaps

Keep warm and cosy in this snuggly hat. The earflaps are decorated with pompoms on strings, but you could leave them plain if you prefer.

You will need

....

1 x 50g ball (75m/81yd) Sirdar Click Chunky with wool (70% acrylic, 30% wool), in each of:

Yarn A: shade 165, blue

Yarn B: shade 142, lamb

5mm crochet hook

Darning needle

Cardboard

A round object with a diameter of 10cm (4in) or a pompom maker

Measurements

....

Finished hat approx 57cm (22½in) unstretched

Tension

....

Approx 12 sts and 9 rows to 10cm (4in) over htr using 5mm hook, or size required to obtain correct tension.

1 Crochet the hat

Using 5mm hook and yarn A, ch2.

Rnd 1: 6htr in first ch made, join into a ring with a sl st.

Rnd 2: Ch2, 2htr in each st around, join with a sl st into top of 2-ch. (12 htr)

Rnd 3: Ch2, 2htr in each st around, join with a sl st into top of 2-ch. (24 htr)

Rnd 4: Ch2, [2htr in next st, 1htr] around, join with a sl st into top of 2-ch. (36 htr)

Rnd 5: Ch2, [2htr in next st, 2htr] around, join with a sl st into top of 2-ch. (48 htr)

Change to yarn B and work 1 rnd straight in dc.

Change back to yarn A.

Rnd 7: Ch2, [2htr in next st, 6htr] around, join with a sl st into top of 2-ch. (54 htr)

Change to yarn B and work 1 rnd straight in dc.

Change back to yarn A.

Work 2 rnds straight in htr.

Change to yarn B.

Work 4 rnds straight in htr.

Change to yarn A and work 3 rows straight in htr.

2 Crochet the earflap

Work straight for earflap as follows:

Row 1: 12htr, turn, leaving rem sts unworked.

Row 2: Htr2tog, htr to last 2 sts, htr2tog, turn. (10 htr)

Rep last row until 4 sts rem.

Fasten off yarn.

Rejoin yarn A to 17th st along from last earflap and work as for first earflap.

Abbreviations (see page 19)

ch chain

dc double crochet

htr half treble

htr2tog half treble crochet 2 together

rep repeat

rem remain

rnd round

sl st slip stitch

Techniques (see pages 10–19)

Fastening off

Making fabric

Turn

Working in the round

NOTE Hat is worked in complete rounds, do not turn throughout.

Earflaps are worked straight in rows, turn at the end of each row.

Yarn is not fastened off after each colour change, and you do not need to join yarn to each new row once it has been joined in. Simply carry the yarn at the back of the work, and pick up and work the new yarn in the next stitch when instructed.

3 Crochet the border

Join yarn B to any point around edge of hat and work a row of dc evenly around entire edge, including earflaps. Do not turn. Work one further row in dc. Fasten off yarn.

4 Finishing

Use the darning needle to weave in the ends. Ask an adult to help you to lightly press the hat with an iron, placing a tea towel on top to protect the yarn if necessary.

5 Make the pompoms

Make two multi-coloured pompoms approx 10cm (4in) diameter, using strands of yarns A and B held together. You can either use a pompom maker or make your own. Draw around something with a diameter of about 10cm (4in) onto two pieces of stiff card or cardboard (a cereal box works well). Draw a smaller circle inside (draw around a large button or a cotton reel). Cut out the larger circle then cut out the inner circle.

Keep the 2 circles held together and wrap the yarn through the ring, wrapping it closely together. Don't wrap it too tightly or it will be difficult to cut. When it is closely packed with yarn all the way around, carefully cut through the wraps of yarn around the edge of the rings. Slide a length of yarn between the rings and tie it tightly with a knot to hold all the strands together.

Remove the rings of the pompom maker and fluff up the pompom. You can trim any straggly ends with scissors to make a neat ball.

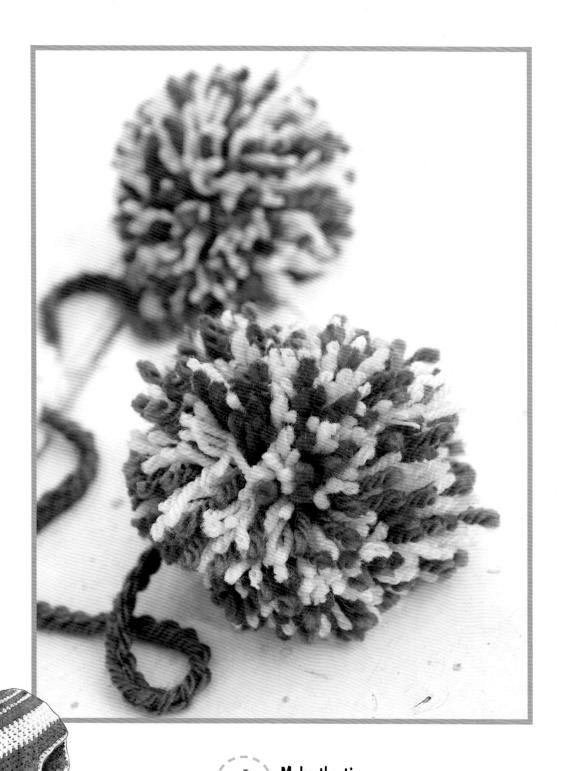

6 Make the ties

Crochet two chains for the ties, approx 50cm (20in) long and attach one to the bottom of each earflap. Sew the pompoms to the ties to finish.

Bootie slippers

Simple slippers — which are easily adaptable for your size of foot — are brilliant for keeping your toes cosy while you watch tv, chat online or do your homework.

You will need

1 x 50g ball (100m/109yd) Rico Essentials Soft Merino Aran (100% merino wool), in each of:

Yarn A: shade 020, light grey

Yarn B: shade 041, eucalyptus

Yarn C: shade 036, royal blue

Yarn D: shade 050, pistachio

Yarn E: shade 037, navy

Paper and pencil

5mm and 2.5mm crochet hooks

Thick wool felt

Darning needle

Measurements

Adjustable to fit your own foot size

Tension

17dc and 16 rows to 10cm (4in) over dc using 5mm hook, or size required to obtain correct tension.

1 **Make the slipper sole**
Draw around your foot onto a piece of paper to get the basic shape and size of the sole – if one foot is larger than the other, draw around the larger one. Round off the shape so that it flows smoothly, and make it symmetrical so that either slipper fits either foot.

2 **Cut out the felt**
Pin your foot template to the felt and cut out two shapes. Punch holes all round the edge of the felt using a sharp needle or the end of your small crochet hook. Space the holes 5mm (¼in) apart and 5mm (¼in) in from the outside edge.

Abbreviations (see page 19)

ch chain

dc double crochet

dc2tog double crochet 2 together

rep repeat

rnd round

sl st slip stitch

Techniques (see pages 10–19)

Decreasing

Fastening off

Joining in a new colour

Making fabric

Sewing up

Starting to work in the round

3 Crochet the slipper

Using the 2.5mm hook and yarn A, make a slip knot. Starting at the hole nearest the centre of the heel, work 1dc in each of the holes around the edge of the felt sole. Join rnd with a sl st to first dc.

Change to 5mm hook.

Rnd 2: Ch1, 1dc in each st around, join with sl st to first dc.

Rep Rnd 2 four more times.

Rnd 7: Work in dc, decreasing 5 sts evenly over toe sts. Change to yarn B and work one row straight in dc without decreasing.

Change to yarn C.

Rnd 9: Work in dc, decreasing 5 sts evenly over toe sts. Change to yarn D and work one row straight in dc without decreasing.

Change to yarn E.

Rnd 11: Work in dc, decreasing 5 sts evenly over toe sts. Fasten off yarn.

4 Finishing

Thread the darning needle with a length of yarn E and sew up the seam from the toe for 5cm (2in) to join the top of the slipper.

No more boring slippers!

Rose book bag

This project uses double crochet throughout and is perfect as a book bag. You can make the flowers included in the pattern, or use any of the other flowers in the book to decorate your bag — try those from the Floral Purse on page 30, too.

You will need

Debbie Bliss Como (90% wool, 10% cashmere):

6 x 50g balls (252m/276yd) in Yarn A: shade 24, silver

1 x 50g ball (42m/46yd) in Yarn B: shade 18, lime

1 x 50g ball (120m/131yd) Rowan Belle Organic DK (50% organic wool, 50% cotton) in Yarn C: shade 004, persimmon

1 x 50g ball (94m/103yd) Rooster Almerino Aran (50% baby alpaca, 50% merino) in Yarn D: shade 306, gooseberry

9mm, 7mm and 4.5mm crochet hooks

Darning needle

Sewing needle and thread

Measurements

Bag approx 34 x 29cm (13½ x 11½in), handles 64cm (25in)

Tension

Exact tension isn't important on this project.

1 **Crochet the bag (make 2 pieces)**
Using 9mm hook and yarn A, ch25.
Next row: Ch1, 1dc to end, turn.
Rep this row until bag measures 32cm (12½in).
Fasten off yarn.

2 **Crochet the edging**
Work around top edge of bag. With the right side facing and using 9mm hook and yarn B, join yarn in a corner st, *ch3, sl st in 3rd ch from hook, miss 1 st, 1dc in next st; rep from * to end.
Sl st into joining st.
Fasten off yarn.

3 **Crochet the handles (make two)**
Using 7mm hook and yarn A, ch5, turn, 1dc in second ch from hook, 1dc to end. (4 sts)
Next row: Ch1, 1dc in each st to end, turn. (4 sts)
Rep this row until handle measures approx 66cm (26in).
Fasten off yarn.

Shopping with style!

Abbreviations (see page 19)

ch chain

ch sp chain space

cont continue

dc double crochet

rep repeat

rnd round

st(s) stitch(es)

sl st slip stitch

tr treble crochet

Techniques (see pages 10–19)

Fastening off

Joining in a new colour

Making fabric

Sewing up

Starting to work in the round

Turn

4 Crochet the flowers (make 4)

Using 4.5mm hook and yarn C, ch4, sl st into first ch to make a ring.

Rnd 1: *1dc, 1tr, 1dc into ring; rep from * 3 more times. (4 petals)

Rnd 2: *Ch2, from wrong side sl st into base of second dc of next petal (pick up 2 loops); rep from * 3 more times. Slip last st into first sl st. (4 loops)

Rnd 3: *4tr in next 2-ch sp, sl st in same ch sp; rep from * 3 more times.
Fasten off yarn.

Rnd 4: Continue in yarn C. Work into back of petals and picking up two loops, join yarn at base of highest point of previous round, *ch3, sl st into middle of base of next petal; rep from * 3 more times, slip last st into joining st.

Rnd 5: *8tr in next 3-ch sp, sl st in next 3-ch sp; rep from * 3 more times, slip last st into joining st.
Fasten off yarn.
Change to yarn D.

Rnd 6: Working into back of petals and picking up two loops, join yarn into middle of base of petal (next 8 tr) of previous round, *ch3, sl st into middle of base of next petal; rep from * 3 more times, slip last st into joining st.

Rnd 7: *10tr in 3-ch sp, sl st in same 3-ch sp; rep from * 3 more times.
Fasten off yarn.

5 Sew the bag

With wrong sides facing, use a darning needle and matching yarn to sew the front and back together with whip stitch, sewing up the side and bottom seams, and leaving the top open.

6 Attach the handles

Place a pin 2.5cm (1in) from each outside seam on the top of the bag as a marker. Position the ends of the handles approx 5cm (2in) down into the bag, aligning the outside edge of the handle with the pin. Stitch the handle in place and repeat on the same side with the other end of the handle (make sure the handle isn't twisted). Repeat for the second handle on the other side of the bag.

7 **Attach the flowers**
Sew each flower to the front of
the bag, just below the handles,
keeping your stitches hidden at the back
of the flower.

CHAPTER 2

Jewellery

Chain necklace

You only need to know how to make a chain to make this fun and colourful necklace. The necklace can be made in any length — you could make shorter ones as bracelets or anklets, or make it longer to wear as a decorative belt. Remember to string all your beads onto the yarn before you start!

You will need

1 x 50g ball (130m/142yd) Rico Essentials Cotton DK (100% mercerized cotton) in shade 01, rose

4mm crochet hook

12 wooden or plastic shaped beads, approx 1–1.5cm (½–¾in) diameter

Measurements

Approx 140cm (55in), but you can make yours to any length

Tension

Exact tension isn't important for this project.

Abbreviations (see page 19)

ch chain

rep repeat

sl st slip stitch

Techniques (see pages 10–19)

Fastening off

1 Thread the beads

Attach the darning needle to the end of the yarn and thread it through 12 beads. Make a slip knot in the yarn end before the beads and place it on the hook.

Beads galore!

You can use any type of bead for your necklace, or why not try tiny buttons or even charms?

2 Crochet the chain

Using 4mm hook, *ch20, bring bead up to hook, ch around bead; rep from * until all beads are used, ch20, sl st in first ch made.

Fasten off the yarn and weave in the ends.

Headband

A basic strip of crochet can be easily turned into a headband, with a cute bow to hide the seam and add extra prettiness.

You will need

1 x 50g ball (175m/191yd) Sirdar Snuggly Kisses DK (55% nylon, 45% acrylic), in shade 0754, pink

3.25mm crochet hook

Darning needle

Measurements

Headband is approx 5.5cm (2¼in) wide and to fit head approx 44(48:52)cm [17¼(19:20½)in] around, although it is easy to adapt to fit your own head

Tension

Approx 21 sts and 14 rows to 10cm (4in) over htr using 3.25mm hook, or size required to obtain correct tension.

1 ### Crochet the headband
Using 3.25mm hook, ch14.
Row 1: 1htr in 2nd ch from hook, then 1htr in each ch to end of row, turn. (12 htr)
Row 2: Ch2, 1htr in each st to end of row, turn.
Rep last row until headband is approx 44(48:52)cm [17¼(19:20½)in] long, or desired head circumference, allowing for stretch.
Fasten off yarn.

2 ### Crochet the bow
Using 3.25mm hook, ch16.
Row 1: 1htr in 2nd ch from hook, then 1htr in each ch to end of row, turn. (14 htr)
Row 2: Ch2, 1htr in each st to end of row, turn.
Rep last row until strip is approx 10cm (4in) long.
Fasten off yarn.

Using 3.25mm hook, ch8.
Row 1: 1htr in 2nd ch from hook, then 1htr in each ch to end of row, turn. (6 htr)
Row 2: Ch2, 1htr in each st to end of row, turn.
Rep last row until strip is approx 11cm (4½in) long.
Fasten off yarn.

Perfect for dance class

3 Sew together

Sew the ends of the headband together to make a circle, using a darning needle and whip stitch.

4 Attach the bow

Position the larger bow strip centred over the seam on the headband and sew it in place in the middle along the edge for about 2.5cm (1in) on each side. Wrap the small bow strip around the centre of the larger bow strip and headband, sewing the ends together at back of the headband to create a gathered bow.

Flowers

It's so easy to work in the round and create fast and simply stunning brooches or hairclips with these pretty flowers. Adorn these little lovelies with buttons or beads for added sparkle.

1 **Crochet the Large daisy**
Using 3.5mm hook and yarn A, ch6 and join into a ring with a sl st.
Rnd 1: 20dc into ring, join rnd with a sl st.
Fasten off yarn A.
Join yarn B to any dc with a sl st.
Rnd 2: Ch20, [sl st in next dc, ch20] around, join last petal to bottom of first ch with a sl st.
Fasten off yarn and weave in ends.
Attach a brooch back, safety pin or hairclip to the back of the flower with a few stitches over and over the fastening, using a sewing needle and thread. You could add buttons or beads to the front, too.

The flowers use very small amounts of yarn, so they're perfect for using up leftovers.

Abbreviations (see page 19)

ch chain

dc double crochet

rep repeat

sl st slip stitch

sp space

tr treble crochet

Techniques (see pages 10–19)

Fastening off

Joining in a new colour

Turn

Sewing on buttons

Starting to work in the round

NOTE Daisies and small flowers are worked in complete rounds, do not turn throughout.

Loopy flower is worked in rows.

② Crochet the Small daisy

Using 3.5mm hook and yarn A, ch6 and join into a ring with a sl st.

Rnd 1: 20dc into ring, join into top of first dc with a sl st. Fasten off yarn A.

Join yarn B to any dc with a sl st.

Rnd 2: Ch10, [miss 1 dc, sl st in next dc, ch10] around, join last petal to bottom of first ch with a sl st. Fasten off yarn and weave in ends.

Attach a brooch back, safety pin or hairclip to the back of the flower with a few stitches over and over the fastening, using a sewing needle and thread. You could add buttons or beads to the front, too.

Crochet the Loopy flower

Using 3.5mm hook and yarn C, ch5.

Row 1: 1dc in 2nd ch from hook, 1dc in each ch to end of row, turn. (4 dc)

Row 2: Ch30, 1dc in dc at base of ch, dc to end of row, turn.

Row 3: Ch1, dc to end of row, turn.

Row 4: Ch30, 1dc in dc at base of ch, dc to end of row, turn.

Rep Rows 3–4 eight times more.

Change to yarn D.

Next row: Ch1, dc to end of row, turn.

Next row: Ch25, 1dc in dc at base of ch, dc to end of row, turn.

Next row: Ch1, dc to end of row, turn.

Rep last two rows 9 times more.

Change to yarn E.

Next row: Ch1, dc to end of row, turn.

Next row: Ch20, 1dc in dc at base of ch, dc to end of row, turn.

Next row: Ch1, dc to end of row, turn.

Rep last two rows 9 times more.

Fasten off yarn.

Roll up strip with smaller loops in the middle and secure in place by sewing together through the dc section at the back.

Attach a brooch back, safety pin or hairclip to the back of the flower with a few stitches over and over the fastening, using a sewing needle and thread.

Crochet the Small flower

Using 3.5mm hook and yarn F, ch3.

Rnd 1: 5dc in first ch, join with a sl st into top of first st.

Rnd 2: 2dc in each st around, join with a sl st into top of first st. (10 dc)

Rnd 3: [1dc, 2dc in next st] around, join with a sl st into top of first st. (15 dc)

Fasten off yarn F.

Join yarn G to any dc with a sl st.

Rnd 4: Ch1, 2tr in each of next 2 sts, [1dc, 2tr in each of next 2 sts] to end of rnd, join with a sl st in top of 1-ch. (5 petals made)

Fasten off yarn and weave in ends.

Attach a brooch back, safety pin or hairclip to the back of the flower with a few stitches over and over the fastening, using a sewing needle and thread. You could add buttons or beads to the front, too.

Heart and star hairclips

Crochet is the perfect way to cover boring hairclips and slides in your favourite colour. Add a cute heart or star to really make them shine.

You will need

1 x 100g ball (280m/306yd) DMC Petra no 3 (100% long staple cotton), in each of:

Yarn A: shade 5321, red

Yarn B: shade 53904, ice blue

Yarn C: shade 53900, green

3.25mm crochet hook

Hairclips

Sewing needle and matching thread

Measurements

One size, hearts and stars approx 2.5cm (1in) wide

Tension

Exact tension isn't important for this project.

1 Crochet the hairclip

Using 3.25mm hook and any colour, join yarn to the point of the hairclip with a sl st.
Work dc round the clip, through the centre hole, to cover it, leaving the broad end unworked.
Fasten off yarn.

2 Crochet the heart

Rnd 1: Ch2, 9dc in 2nd ch from hook, join into a ring with a sl st.
Rnd 2: Ch1, 1dc in next st, [1htr, 5tr, 1htr] all into next st, sl st in next st, [1htr, 5tr, 1htr] all into next st, dc to end of rnd, join with a sl st into first ch.
Fasten off yarn.

3 Crochet the star

Rnd 1: Ch2, 10dc in 2nd ch from hook, join with a sl st into top of 2-ch.
Rnd 2: [Ch2, 1tr in next st, ch2, sl st in next st] 5 times.
Fasten off yarn.

Accessorize with cute clips

Abbreviations (see page 19)

ch chain

dc double crochet

htr half treble crochet

sl st slip stitch

st stitch

tr treble crochet

Techniques (see pages 10–19)

Fastening off

4 Finish the hairclip

Sew the heart or star to the wide end of the clip to hide the uncovered part, using a sewing needle and matching sewing thread.

Bracelets

These simple bracelet tubes can be adapted to fit you perfectly. Make lots of them in different colours to go with all your favourite clothes.

You will need

1 x 50g ball (95m/104yd) Sirdar Snuggly Baby Bamboo (80% bamboo, 20% wool), in each of:

Yarn A: shade 162, toy box red

Yarn B: shade 160, paint box pink

Yarn C: shade 161, baby berries purple

Yarn D: shade 159, jack-in-the-box turquoise

3.5mm crochet hook

Stitch marker

Darning needle

Measurements

To fit you!

Tension

Exact tension isn't important for this project.

1 Crochet the bracelet

Using 3.5mm hook and any yarn, ch8, join into a ring with a sl st into top of first ch.

Rnd 1: Ch1, 1dc (blo) in each ch around, do not join rnd.

Rnd 2: 1dc (blo) in each ch around, do not join rnd.

Rep last rnd until bracelet measures approx 18cm (7in), or length to fit your wrist allowing for stretch over hand.
Fasten off yarn.

2 Finishing the bracelet

Thread the tail end of the yarn onto a darning needle and sew the two open ends together neatly to form a circle.

Groovy bracelets for every day!

Abbreviations (see page 19)

blo back loop only

ch chain

dc double crochet

rep repeat

sl st slip stitch

Techniques (see pages 10–19)

Fastening off

Marking rounds with a stitch marker

Starting to work in the round

NOTE Bracelets are worked in continuous spiral rounds, do not turn throughout and do not join rounds.

Felted cherry brooch

These cherries are very quick and really cute. They are small and a little bit fiddly, but the stitch is very simple – so once you've mastered crocheting in the round, give them a go.

You will need

1 x 100g hank (200m/220yd) Cascade 220 DK (100% Peruvian wool) in each of:

Yarn A: shade 8414, bright red

Yarn B: shade 0980, pesto

3.5mm crochet hook

Darning needle

Sewing needle and thread

Small brooch pin

Measurements

Approx 7cm (2¾in) wide x 7.5cm (3in) long

Tension

Exact tension isn't important on this project.

1 Crochet the cherries (make two)
Using 3.5mm hook and yarn A, ch2.

Rnd 1: 6dc in second ch from hook.
Rnd 2: 2dc in each st. (12 dc)
Rnd 3: 1dc in each st. (12 dc)
Stuff cherry with scraps of red yarn.
Rnd 4: Dc2tog around. (6 dc)
Continue to dc2tog until hole closes.
Fasten off yarn and weave in ends.

2 Crochet the stalk (make one)
Using 3.5mm hook and yarn B, ch20.
Fasten off yarn.

3 Crochet the leaves (make two)
Using 3.5mm hook and yarn B, ch8, sl st in second ch from hook, 1dc, 1htr, 1tr, 1htr, 1dc, sl st in last ch.
Working on other side of ch, sl st in second ch from hook, 1dc in next st, 1htr, 1tr, 1htr, 1dc, sl st.
Fasten off yarn.

Abbreviations (see page 19)

ch chain

dc double crochet

dc2tog double crochet 2 together

htr half treble crochet

rnd round

sl st slip stitch

Techniques (see pages 10–19)

Fastening off

Starting to work in the round

So sweet and easy!

4 Sew the cherry

Using a darning needle and matching yarn, sew one end of the stalk to each cherry. Find the centre of the stalk and sew the leaves to the top.

To felt well, the cherries must be made in 100% wool.

5 Felting

Ask an adult to help you use the washing machine. Put the cherries in a pillowcase or laundry bag and wash in the washing machine on a hot wash, twice (include a large towel or two to help). When felted, the wool will be thicker and the crochet will have shrunk a little. Let the brooch dry.

Finish the brooch

6 Attach a brooch pin to the back of the leaves using a sewing needle and thread. Take a few stitches over and over the fastening, making sure that you can't see the stitches or the brooch pin from the front.

Princess tiara

A simple-to-make tiara fit for any little princess. We've sewn on pearls, but you can use beads or sew-on jewels if you prefer.

You will need

1 x 20g ball (150m/164yd) DMC Metallic Crochet Thread (60% viscose, 40% metallized polyester), in shade L168, silver

2.75mm crochet hook

Darning needle

Headband

Beads for embellishment

Beading or thin sewing needle and thread

Measurements

Headband to fit wearer's head; crocheted section is approx 2cm (¾in) high

Tension

Exact tension isn't important for this project.

1 Crochet the tiara

Using 2.75mm hook, attach yarn to headband and work 42dc around the centre section of the headband, turn.

Next row: 1dc, [ch5, miss 3 sts, 1dc in next st] 5 times, ch6, miss 4 sts, 1dc in next st, ch7, miss 5 sts, 1dc in next st, ch6, miss 4 sts, 1dc in next st, [ch5, miss 3 sts, 1dc in next st] 5 times, turn.

Next row: [7dc in next 5-ch sp, sl st in dc] 5 times, 9dc in next ch sp, sl st in dc, 11dc in next ch sp, sl st in dc, 9dc in next ch sp, sl st in dc [7dc in next 5-ch sp, sl st in dc] 5 times.
Fasten off yarn.

2 Adding beads

If you'd like to add some extra jewels to your tiara you can attach beads to the crochet. Thread a beading or sewing needle with thread and knot the end. Bring the needle out in the position where you would like your bead. Thread a bead onto the needle and down the thread. Take the needle back in close to where it emerged, so that the bead sits on the headband. Take a few more stitches through the bead to secure it.

Abbreviations (see page 19)

ch chain

ch sp chain space

dc double crochet

rep repeat

sl st slip stitch

sp space

Techniques (see pages 10–19)

Fastening off

Turn

For a simple version, simply work a row of double crochet then finish off.

CHAPTER 3

Bedroom Essentials

Floral curtain tie-backs

These curtain ties use very little yarn, so you can use up scraps of any type leftover from another project. Simply fasten them over a hook behind the curtains to add some pretty styling to your bedroom.

You will need

1 x 50g ball (110m/120yd) Debbie Bliss Cashmerino DK (55% merino wool, 33% microfibre, 12% cashmere) in Yarn A: shade 011, green

1 x 50g ball (112.5m/124yd) Rooster Almerino DK (50% baby alpaca, 50% merino wool) in Yarn B: shade 211, Brighton Rock

4mm crochet hook

Darning needle

Measurements

Makes two tie-backs each approx 110cm (43in) long

Tension

Exact tension isn't important for this project.

1 Crochet the petal flowers (make 10)

Using 4mm hook and yarn A, ch6, join with sl st into first ch.
Make 16dc into ring, joining tail into each dc around ring, join with a sl st into top of first st.
Change to yarn B.
*Ch3, 1tr in each of next 2 sts, ch3, sl st in next st; rep from * 4 more times. (5 petals)
Fasten off yarn.
Pull tail to close up centre hole and sew in ends.

2 Crochet the small roses (make 4)

Using 4mm hook and yarn B, ch48.
Petals 1–3: Miss 3 ch, 1tr in each of next 2 ch, ch2, sl st in next ch, *ch3, 1tr in each of next 2 ch, ch2, sl st in next ch; rep from * to end once more. (3 petals)
Petals 4–6: *Ch4, 1dtr in each of next 4 ch, ch3, sl st in next ch; rep from * twice more.
Petals 7–9: *Ch4, 1dtr in each of next 6 ch, ch3, sl st in next ch; rep from * twice more.
Fasten off yarn.

Abbreviations (see page 19)

ch chain

dc double crochet

dtr double treble

rep repeat

st(s) stitch(es)

sl st slip stitch

tr treble

trtr triple treble

Techniques (see pages 10–19)

Fastening off

Turn

NOTE Each tie-back has two small roses, one large rose and five petal flowers.

3 Crochet the large roses (make 2)

Using 4mm hook and yarn B, ch99.

Petals 1–4: Miss 3 ch, 1tr in each of next 2 ch, ch2, sl st in next ch, [ch3, 1tr in each of next 2 ch, ch2, sl st in next ch] 3 times.

Petals 5–8: [Ch4, 1dtr in each of next 4 ch, ch3, sl st in next ch] 4 times.

Petals 9–12: [Ch4, 1dtr in each of next 6 ch, ch3, sl st in next ch] 4 times.

Petals 13–16: [Ch5, 1trtr in each of next 8 ch, ch4, sl st in next ch] 4 times.

Fasten off yarn.

4 Make up the roses

To make roses, ask an adult to help you press the petals flat with an iron. Starting with smaller petals, coil the petals round, keeping the base flat at the chain edge, and stitch in place as you go.

5 Make the tie-back chain

Using yarn A, make two lengths of chain for each tie-back, each 54cm (21in) long.
Fasten off yarn.

6 Attach the flowers

Attach one end of one chain to the back of one small rose, leave a 10cm (4in) gap then attach the chain to the back of a large rose. Make a 2.5cm (1in) loop at other end of chain and stitch it in place.

7 Join the tie-back chains

Attach one end of the second chain to the back of the other small rose. Leave a 7.5cm (3in) gap and cross the second chain over the first chain on the back of the large rose. Attach in place, so the chains are secured and crossed at the back. Make a 2.5cm (1in) loop at the other end of the second chain and stitch it in place.

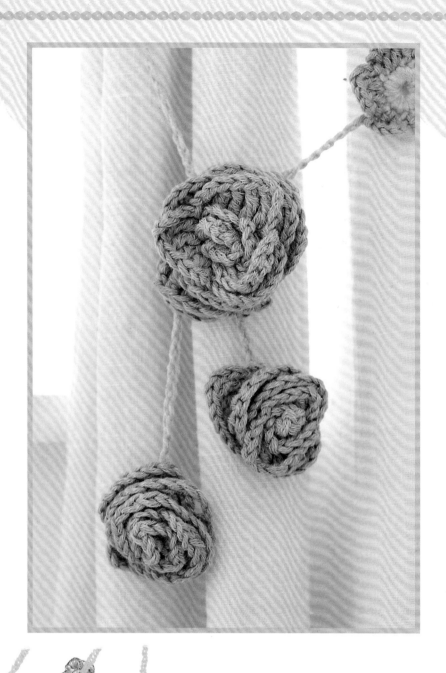

8 Attach the petal flowers

Place five petal flowers along the chains where they will be visible, leaving a 2.5cm (1in) gap between each. Sew the petal flowers to the chain. Use the loops to attach the tie-back to a hook. Repeat steps 5 to 8 to make the second tie-back.

Storage jars

Make these covers for jars, vases and tins to store pens, pencils, crochet hooks — or fill them with water to display flowers with colourful style.

You will need

1 x 50g ball (112m/120yd) Artesano Soft Merino Superwash DK (100% merino superwash), in each of:

Yarn A: shade 1291, sea blue

Yarn B: shade 5167, teal

Yarn C: shade 2083, fuchsia

Yarn D: shade 6315, lime green

Yarn E: shade SFN10, cream

Yarn F: shade 7254, sand yellow

3.5mm crochet hook

Darning needle

Assorted jars and containers

Measurements

To fit tubular storage containers of approx 5cm, 7cm and 9cm (2in, 2¾in and 3½in) in diameter, and of any height

Tension

Approx 18 sts and 26 rows to 10cm (4in) in dc using 3.5mm hook, or size required to obtain correct tension.

1 Crochet the cover

Begin all jars from Rnd 1. For 5cm (2in) jar, work to Rnd 5 and then work from the all sizes instruction; for 7cm (2¾in) jar, work to Rnd 7 and then work from all sizes instruction; and for 9cm (3½in) jar, work all rows before completing from all sizes instruction.

Begin with yarn A and then work 1 or 2 row stripes alternately of all colours.

Using 3.5mm hook and yarn A, ch2.

Rnd 1: 6dc in first ch, join into a ring with a sl st.

Rnd 2: 2dc in each st around, join with a sl st into top of first st. (12 dc)

Rnd 3: [1dc, 2dc in next st] around. (18 dc)

Rnd 4: [2dc, 2dc in next st] around. (24 dc)

Rnd 5: [3dc, 2dc in next st] around. (30 dc)

Rnd 6: [4dc, 2dc in next st] around. (36 dc)

Rnd 7: [5dc, 2dc in next st] around. (42 dc)

Rnd 8: [6dc, 2dc in next st] around, join with a sl st into top of first st. (48 dc)

Rnd 9: [7dc, 2dc in next st] around, join rnd with a sl st. (54 dc)

Rnd 10: [8dc, 2dc in next st] around, join rnd with a sl st. (60 dc)

All sizes

Next rnd: Ch1, 1dc in each st around, join rnd with a sl st. Continue straight in dc on these sts until desired height of jar is reached, striping as you wish.

Fasten off yarn.

Keep your pencils tidy!

blo back loop only

ch chain

dc double crochet

rnd round

sl st slip stitch

Techniques (see pages 10–19)

Fastening off

Joining in a new colour

Starting to work in the round

NOTE Pieces are worked in the round, do not turn throughout.

2 Finishing the cover

Use the darning needle to weave in the loose ends on the wrong side, then turn the cover right side out.

3 Cover your jar

Slip the crocheted 'cosy' over a jar or vase and fill with pens and pencils or a pretty bunch of flowers.

Zigzag bolster

A crazily striped bolster for your bed. Have fun mixing and matching all your favourite colours.

1 **Crochet the bolster**

Using 4mm hook and yarn A, ch98.

Row 1: 2dc in 2nd ch from hook, *1dc in each of next 7 ch, miss 1 ch, 1dc in each of next 7 ch, 3dc in next ch; rep from * to end, but work 2dc in last ch instead of 3dc, turn.

Row 2: Ch1, 2dc in first st, *7dc, miss next 2 dc, 7dc, 3dc in next stitch; rep from * to end, but work 2dc in last st instead of 3dc, turn.

Rep Row 2 for pattern, changing colour after every four rows, until work measures approx 48cm (19in) long.

Fasten off yarn.

2 **Sew together**

Weave in the ends. Sew the piece together along the two long edges, fitting the peaks and troughs of the zigzag into each other, using a darning needle and whip stitch and a matching yarn.

Soft, cosy and funky!

You will need

1 x 50g ball (95m/104yd) Sirdar Snuggly Baby Bamboo (80% bamboo, 20% wool), in each of:

Yarn A: shade 144, tom thumb green

Yarn B: shade 157, yellow submarine

Yarn C: shade 149, scooter blue

Yarn D: shade 159, jack-in-the-box turquoise

Yarn E: shade 161, baby berries purple

Yarn F: shade 160, paint box pink

Yarn G: shade 162, toy box red

Yarn H: shade 126, rocking horse red

Yarn I: shade 134, babe pink

4mm crochet hook

Darning needle

Toy stuffing, or bolster pad measuring 39cm (15½in) long and 49cm (19½in) in circumference

½m (½yd) fabric

A round object to draw around, like a plate, about 15cm (6in) in diameter

Fabric marker pen

Sewing needle and matching thread

Measurements

Approx 36cm (14in) wide

Tension

15 sts and 15 rows to 10cm (4in) in zigzag pattern using 4mm hook, or size required to obtain correct tension.

4 Sew the end

Fold the edge of the fabric circles over to the wrong side by about 1cm (½in) and ask an adult to help you press them with an iron. Sew a circle of fabric to one end of the bolster using a sewing needle and thread and small overstitches.

3 Cut out the fabric

Put a plate or a round object of about 15cm (6in) in diameter on the wrong side of your fabric and draw round it to make two circles. Cut the circles out carefully.

5 Finish the bolster

Either fill the bolster with toy stuffing until it is firm or insert a bolster pad. Sew the remaining circle of fabric to the open end of the bolster as you did in step 4.

Colourful bowl

This small bowl can be used to hold items on your dresser or desk, like jewellery, paper clips, hairclips or tiny toys. You could even make several bowls in different colours to liven up your room!

You will need

1 x 50g ball (120m/131yd) Patons Diploma Gold DK (55% wool, 25% acrylic, 20% nylon) in Yarn A: shade 06125, apple green

Small amount of Stylecraft Special DK (100% acrylic) in Yarn B: shade 1068, turquoise

3.5mm crochet hook

Stitch marker

Darning needle

Measurements

Our bowl measured about 10cm (4in); however, the bowl can be made in any size

Tension

Exact tension isn't important for this project.

1 **Crochet the bowl**
Using 3.5mm hook and yarn A, ch2, 6dc in 2nd ch from hook.
Rnd 1: 2dc in each dc. (12 sts)
Rnd 2: *1dc in first dc, 2dc in next dc; rep from * to end. (18 sts)
Rnd 3: *1dc in each of next 2 dc, 2dc in next dc; rep from * to end. (24 sts)
Rnd 4: *1dc in each of next 3 dc, 2dc in next dc; rep from * to end. (30 sts)
Rnd 5: *1dc in each of next 4 dc, 2dc in next dc; rep from * to end. (36 sts)
Rnd 6: *1dc in each of next 5 dc, 2dc in next dc; rep from * to end. (42 sts)
Rnd 7: *1dc in each of next 6 dc, 2dc in next dc; rep from * to end. (48 sts)

Rnd 8: *1dc in each of next 7 dc, 2dc in next dc; rep from * to end. (54 sts)
Rnd 9: *1dc in each of next 8 dc, 2dc in next dc; rep from * to end. (60 sts)
Rnd 10: *1dc in each of next 9 dc, 2dc in next dc; rep from * to end. (66 sts)
Rnds 11–15: 1dc in each dc. (66 sts)
Change to yarn B.
Rnds 16–17: 1dc in each dc. (66 sts)
Fasten off yarn. Use the darning needle to weave in the tail ends.

Stylish storage for all your bits and bobs!

This project is made in the round; be sure to use a stitch marker to mark the first stitch of the round throughout.

Knickerbocker glory bunting

Bunting is a lovely, happy way to brighten up your bedroom or you could string it up in the garden or kitchen for a birthday celebration in style!

You will need

1 x 50g ball (112m/123yd) King Cole Merino Blend DK (100% merino wool) in each of:

shade 5, sky

shade 55, gold

shade 94, dusky pink

shade 787, fuchsia

1 x 50g ball (110m/120yd) Debbie Bliss Cashmerino DK (55% merino wool, 33% microfibre, 12% cashmere) in each of:

shade 017, lilac

shade 029, light green

1 x 50g ball (120m/131yd) Rowan Belle Organic DK (50% organic wool, 50% cotton) in shade 004, persimmon

4mm crochet hook

Darning needle

Measurements

Each flag approx 18cm (7in) across top edge

Tension

Exact tension isn't important for this project.

1 Crochet the flags

Make 6, or as many as required, in different colours with contrast edgings.

Using 4mm hook and flag main colour, ch26.

Row 1: 1dc in 2nd ch from hook, 1dc in each ch to end, turn. (25 sts)

Row 2: Ch1, dc2tog, 1dc in each st to end, turn.

Rep row 2 until 2 sts remain, dc2tog.

Fasten off yarn.

2 Crochet the edging

With right sides facing, join in first contrast colour into top right corner st, ch 3, make 24tr along top edge.

Fasten off yarn.

With right sides facing, join next contrast colour in top left corner, ch1, work 26dc along first side, 3dc in corner st, 26dc along other side ending with a sl st into top of first st.

Fasten off yarn.

Join the flags

3 With a contrasting colour, ch70. With right sides facing, join ch to first flag with sl st in right-hand corner, ch1, *1dc in between each tr across top of flag to end, join next flag with sl st into top right-hand corner; rep from * to end for each flag, sl st into last corner st of last flag. Ch70. Fasten off yarn.

Abbreviations (see page 19)

ch chain

dc double crochet

dc2tog double crochet 2 together

rep repeat

rnd round

sl st slip stitch

st(s) stitch(es)

tr treble

Techniques (see pages 10–19)

Fastening off

Joining in a new colour

Turn

Sew in the ends

4 Using a darning needle at the back of the bunting, stitch to secure the joins in between each flag using the loose ends of wool. Ask an adult to help you to press each flag gently with an iron.

Party time!

Sausage dog draught excluder

Keep your bedroom cosy on cold winter evenings by placing this dog by your door to stop draughts coming under it, or fill the dog with PVC beanbag granules and use him as a doorstop.

You will need

1 x 50g ball (75m/81yd) Sirdar Click Chunky with wool, (70% acrylic, 30% wool), in each of:

Yarn A: shade 148, bud

Yarn B: shade 163, really red

Yarn C: shade 171, blueberry

5mm crochet hook

Toy stuffing

Red felt for ears, legs, tail and nose

White felt for eyes

Buttons for eyes

Sewing needle and thread

Darning needle

Measurements

Approx 68.5cm (27in) long

Tension

Exact tension isn't important for this project but make sure that you crochet tightly so that the stuffing does not show.

1 Crochet the dog

Using 5mm hook and yarn A, ch2.

Rnd 1: 6dc in first ch made, join with a sl st into top of first st.

Rnd 2: 2dc in each dc around, join with a sl st into top of first st. (12 dc)

Rnd 3: [2dc in next st, 1dc] around, join with a sl st into top of first st. (18 dc)

Rnd 4: [2dc in next st, 2dc] around, join with a sl st into top of first st. (24 dc)

Rnd 5: [2dc in next st, 3dc] around, join with a sl st into top of first st. (30 dc)

Rnd 6: [2dc in next st, 4dc] around, join with a sl st into top of first st. (36 dc)

Rnd 7: [2dc in next st, 5dc] around, join with a sl st into top of first st. (42 dc)

Rnd 8: [2dc in next st, 6dc] around, join with a sl st into top of first st. (48 dc)

Work 4 rows straight in dc without increasing.

Change to yarn B and work 2 rows straight.

Change to yarn C and work 2 rows straight.

Change to yarn A and work 2 rows straight.

Cont straight on these 48 sts until dog is approx 68.5cm (27in) long, striping as established, then if necessary, change back to yarn A.

Stuff the body through the open end, with the hook still attached, and then begin to decrease as follows:

Rnd 1: [Dc2tog, 6dc] around, join with a sl st into first st. (42 dc)

Rnd 2: [Dc2tog, 5dc] around, join with a sl st into first st. (36 dc)

Rnd 3: [Dc2tog, 4dc] around, join with a sl st into first st. (30 dc)

Rnd 4: [Dc2tog, 3dc] around, join with a sl st into first st. (24 dc)

Rnd 5: [Dc2tog, 2dc] around, join with a sl st into first st. (18 dc)

Rnd 6: [Dc2tog, 1dc] around, join with a sl st into first st. (12 dc)

Rnd 7: [Dc2tog] around, join with a sl st into first st. (6 dc)

Fasten off yarn and sew up final hole to secure.

Abbreviations (see page 19)

ch chain

dc double crochet

dc2tog double crochet 2 together

rep repeat

rnd round

sl st slip stitch

Techniques (see pages 10–19)

Decreasing

Fastening off

Joining in a new colour

Sewing on buttons

Starting to work in the round

2 **Make the features**
Make a paper template for the ear and leg shapes, drawing them freehand. Cut out the template and pin it to the red felt and cut out two ears and four legs. Cut a thin, pointed strip for the tail.

3 Sew on the features

Using a sewing needle and matching thread, sew the ears to the side of the head using small stitches and hiding the end of the thread in the crochet. Do the same to sew on the legs, placing them on opposite sides at the top and bottom of the dog. Attach the tail so that it points up and is wagging!

4 Sew the eyes

Draw around something round, such as a cotton reel or button, or cut out two circles freehand for the eyes. Sew them to the face and then add two small buttons – you can give your dog a funny expression by sewing the pupils in different places.

5 Sew the nose and mouth

Cut a small triangle of red felt for the nose and sew it in place. Use a leftover piece of red yarn and a darning needle to sew the mouth using backstitch.

A stripy sausage dog just for you!

Round stripy cushion cover

Crochet is perfect for making circles and this cushion cover is a great beginner's project using a rainbow of lovely yarns that would look great in any bedroom.

You will need

1 x 50g ball (90m/98yd) Rowan Belle Organic Aran (50% organic wool, 50% cotton) in each of:

Yarn A: shade 209, Robin's Egg

Yarn B: shade 203, Orchid

Yarn C: shade 205, Rose

Yarn D: shade 212, Zinc

Yarn E: shade 206, Poppy

Yarn F: shade 211, Cilantro

5mm crochet hook

Darning needle

40cm (16in) round cushion pad

Measurements

To fit a 40cm (16in) diameter round cushion pad

Tension

14tr by 8 rows over a 10cm (4in) square using 5mm hook, or size required to obtain correct tension.

1 Crochet the cover (make 2 sides)

Using 5mm hook and yarn A, ch6, join into a ring with sl st into first ch.

Rnd 1: Ch3 (counts as first tr), 11tr into ring, join with a sl st into top of first 3-ch.

Change to yarn B.

Rnd 2: Ch3, 1tr in same st, 2tr in every st to end of round, join with a sl st into top of first 3-ch. (24 sts)

Change to yarn C.

Rnd 3: Ch3, 1tr in same st, *1tr in next st, 2tr in each of next 2 sts; rep from * to last 2 sts, 1tr in next st, 2tr in last st, join with a sl st into top of first 3-ch. (40 sts)

Change to yarn D.

Rnd 4: Ch3, 1tr in same st, *1tr in each of next 3 sts, 2tr in next st; rep from *to last 3 sts, 1tr in each of last 3 sts, join with a sl st into top of first 3-ch. (50 sts)

Change to yarn E.

Rnd 5: Ch3, 1tr in same st, *1tr in each of next 4 sts, 2tr in next st; rep from * to last 4 sts, 1tr in each of last 4 sts, join with sl st

Abbreviations (see page 19)

ch chain

dc double crochet

sl st slip stitch

st(s) stitches

tr treble

Techniques (see pages 10–19)

Fastening off

Making fabric

Starting to work in the round

into top of first 3-ch. (60 sts)
Change to yarn F.

Rnd 6: Ch3, 1tr in same st, *1tr in each of next 5 sts, 2tr in next st; rep from *to last 5 sts, 1tr in each of last 5 sts, join with a sl st into top of first 3-ch. (70 sts)
Change to yarn A.

Rnd 7: Ch3, 1tr in same st, *1tr in each of next 6 sts, 2tr in next st; rep from * to last 6 sts, 1tr in each of last 6 sts, join with a sl st into top of first 3-ch. (80 sts)
Change to yarn B.

Rnd 8: Ch3, 1tr in same st, *1tr in each of next 7 sts, 2tr in next st; rep from *to last 7 sts, 1tr in each of last 7 sts, join with a sl st into top of first 3-ch. (90 sts)
Change to yarn C.

Rnd 9: Ch3, 1tr in same st, *1tr in each of next 8 sts, 2tr in next st; rep from * to last 8 sts, 1tr in each of last 8 sts, join with a sl st into top of first 3-ch. (100 sts)
Change to yarn D.

Rnd 10: As Rnd 5. (120 sts)
Change to yarn E.

Rnd 11: Ch3, 1tr in same st, *1tr in each of next 11 tr, 2tr in next st; rep from * to last 11 tr, 1tr in each of last 11 tr, join with a sl st into top of first 3-ch. (130 sts)
Change to yarn F.

Rnd 12: Ch3, 1tr in same st, *1tr in each of next 12 tr, 2tr in next st; rep from * to last 12 tr, 1tr in each of last 12 tr, join with a sl st into top of first 3-ch.

Change to yarn A.

Rnd 13: As Rnd 7.
Change to yarn B.

Rnd 14: Ch3, 1tr in same st, *1tr in each of next 15 tr, 2tr in next st, rep from * to last 15 tr, 1tr in each of last 15 tr, join with a sl st into top of first 3-ch.
Change to yarn C.

Rnd 15: Ch3, 1tr in same st, *1tr in each of next 16 tr, 2tr in next st; rep from * to last 16 tr, 1tr in each of last 16 tr, join with a sl st into top of first 3-ch.
Change to yarn D.

Rnd 16: As Rnd 9.
Fasten off yarn.

2 Sew together

Put the cushion pieces together with wrong sides facing. Insert the hook into both sides and, using yarn A, make 1 ch. Make 1dc into each st, putting hook through both sides and joining sides together. Leave a big enough gap to push through the cushion pad.

3 Insert the cushion pad

With the hook and yarn still attached, carefully insert the cushion pad through the gap. Continue to crochet in dc until the seam is fully joined together. Fasten off yarn. Weave in ends.

Perfect Gifts

Baby bouncers

Little crochet balls for tiny hands — lovely for babies to hold, throw or crawl after. These are great to practise crocheting in the round. The instructions are for making them in one colour but you could make them stripy if you feel like it.

You will need

Small amounts of each of (choose one colour for a plain ball or combine them to make fun stripes):

King Cole Merino Blend DK (100% merino wool) in shade 55, gold and shade 787, fuchsia

Debbie Bliss Cashmerino DK (55% merino wool, 33% microfibre, 12% cashmere) in: shade 017, lilac and shade 029, light green

Rowan Belle Organic DK (50% organic wool, 50% cotton) in shade 014, robin's egg

Rooster Almerino DK (50% baby alpaca, 50% merino wool) in shade 203, strawberry cream

4mm crochet hook

Stitch marker

Toy stuffing

Measurements

7cm (2¾in) diameter

Tension

Exact tension isn't important for this project.

1 Crochet the ball

Rnd 1: Using 4mm hook and any yarn, ch2, 6dc in second ch from hook.

Rnd 2: 2dc in each st. (12 sts)

Rnd 3: *1dc in next st, 2dc; rep from * to end. (18 sts)

Rnd 4: *1dc in each of next 2 sts, 2dc; rep from * to end. (24 sts)

Rnd 5: *1dc in each of next 3 sts, 2dc; rep from * to end. (30 sts)

Rnds 6–10: 1dc in each st. (30 sts)

Rnd 11: *1dc in each of next 3 sts, dc2tog; rep from * to end. (24 sts)

Rnd 12: *1dc in each of next 2 sts, dc2tog; rep from * to end. (18 sts)

Rnd 13: *1dc in next st, dc2tog; rep from * to end. (12 sts)

Stuff the ball through the opening with small amounts of toy stuffing, until it is well shaped and firm.

Rnd 14: Dc2tog around until hole closes.

Fasten off yarn.

Use the darning needle to sew in the ends.

Playtime for baby

Cheryl the snail

Cheryl makes a great addition to your cuddly toy collection. If you'd like to crochet her as a gift for a little baby or toddler, replace the safety eyes with pompoms or stitch them on using a few stitches of black yarn.

You will need

1 x 50g ball (112m/124yd) Rooster Almerino DK (50% baby alpaca, 50% merino wool) in each of:

Yarn A: shade 207, gooseberry

Yarn B: shade 203, strawberry cream

Small amount of Rowan Pure Wool DK (100% superwash wool), in Yarn C: shade 032, gilt

4mm crochet hook

Pair of safety eyes

Toy stuffing

Measurements

Approx 12.5cm (5in) tall

Tension

Exact tension isn't important for this project but make sure that you crochet tightly so that the stuffing does not show.

1 Crochet the head, body and tail (make all as one)

Begin at the tail end. Using 4mm hook and yarn A, ch2.

Row 1: 1dc in second ch from hook, turn.

Row 2: Ch1, 2dc in next st, turn.

Row 3: Ch1, 2dc in each st, turn. (4 sts)

Row 4: Ch1, 2dc in first st, 1dc in each of next 2 sts, 2dc in last st, turn. (6 sts)

Row 5: Ch1, 1dc in each of next 2 sts, 2dc in next st, 1dc in next 3 sts, sl st into first chain. (7 sts)

Rnd 1: 2dc in each st. (14 sts)

Rnds 2–9: 1dc in each st. (14 sts)

Rnds 10–11: 1dc in each of next 4 sts, sl st in next 6 sts, 1dc in next 4 sts.

Rnds 12–21: 1dc in each st. (14 sts)

Insert the eyes and secure them with a few stitches. Stuff the body firmly with small amounts of toy stuffing, keeping the tail flat

and the body in the upright position. Use the end of a pencil or the blunt end of a crochet hook to push the stuffing in well.

Rnd 22: 1dc in each of next 2 sts, dc2tog, 1dc in each of next 2 sts, dc2tog, 1dc in each of next 2 sts, dc2tog, 1dc in each of last 2 sts. (11 sts)

Rnd 23: 1dc in each of next 2 sts, dc2tog, 1dc in each of next 2 sts, dc2tog, 1dc in each of last 3 sts. (9 sts)

Rnd 24: Dc2tog, 4 times, 1dc in last dc. (5 sts)

Fasten off yarn.

Abbreviations (see page 19)

ch chain

dc double crochet

dc2tog double crochet 2 together

htr(s) half treble(s)

rep repeat

rnd(s) round(s)

sl st slip stitch

st(s) stitch(es)

Techniques (see pages 10–19)

Fastening off

Sewing on buttons

Starting to work in the round

The cutest snail you'll meet!

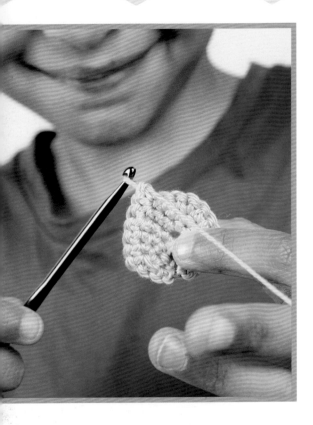

2 Crochet the shell

Using 4mm hook and yarn B, ch2.

Rnd 1: 6dc in second ch from hook.

Rnd 2: 2dc in each st. (12 sts)

Rnd 3: *1dc in next st, 2dc in next st; rep from * to end. (18 sts)

Rnd 4: *1dc in each of next 2 sts, 2dc in next st; rep from * to end. (24 sts)

Rnd 5: *1dc in each of next 3 sts, 2dc in next st; rep from * to end. (30 sts)

Rnds 6–8: 1dc in each st.

Rnd 9: 1dc in each of next 3 sts, dc2tog; rep from * to end. (24 sts)

Rnd 10: *1dc in each of next 2 sts, dc2tog; rep from * to end. (18 sts)

Rnd 11: 1dc in each st.

With the hook still attached, stuff the shell firmly with small amounts of toy stuffing.

Rnd 12: *1dc in next st, dc2tog; rep from * to end. (12 sts)

Rnd 13: Dc2tog to end. (12 sts)

Rnd 14: Miss 1 st, 1dc in next st; rep from * to end.

Fasten off yarn.

Pin and sew the shell to the body by attaching the left side of the shell to the upper right side of the body, and the base of the shell to the top of the lower part of the body.

You could also try making a stripy shell or just crochet the body and antennae to make a cuddly caterpillar!

3 Crochet the antennae (make 2)

Using 4mm hook and yarn C, ch7,
2htr in second ch from hook, sl st in
each ch to end.
Fasten off yarn.
Pin and sew the antennae to either side of
the head.

4 Add the mouth

Using yarn B, sew two curving
straight stitches between the eyes
for a sweet, smiling mouth.

Egg cosies

Keep your boiled eggs warm with these cute little cosies. Quick to make in the round and using bright yarn, they are perfect gifts or breakfast table treats. These are a great way to learn to crochet in the round. To make them even prettier you can add a different coloured border, or to add beads follow the instructions in step 2.

You will need

1 x 50g ball (120m/131yd) Rowan Belle Organic DK (50% organic wool, 50% cotton) in each of:

shade 012, tomato

shade 009, hibiscus

shade 014, robin's egg

shade 016, cilantro

1 x 50g ball (112m/124yd) Rooster Almerino DK (50% baby alpaca, 50% merino wool) in shade 10, custard

3.5mm crochet hook

Darning needle

Sewing needle and thread

6cm (2½in) length x 1.5cm (½in) wide ribbon for each cosy

15 beads (optional)

Measurements

15.5cm (6in) circumference

Tension

Exact tension isn't important for this project.

 1 Crochet the cosy (without beads)

Using 3.5mm hook and your chosen colour, ch2, 6dc in second ch from hook.

Rnd 1: 2dc in each st to end. (12 sts)
Rnd 2: 2dc in each st to end. (24 sts)
Rnds 3–7: 1dc in each st.
Rnd 8: *1dc, dc2tog; rep from * to end. (16 sts)
If using a contrasting colour for the border, fasten off here and rejoin new colour into fastened-off st.
Rnd 9: 1dc in each st, sl st in last st.
Fasten off yarn.
Turn cosy right side out.

2 Crochet the cosy with beads

Thread 15 beads onto the yarn before starting the cosy by threading the yarn onto a needle and passing the needle through the beads.
Rep Rnds 1–8 of cosy pattern.

Beaded rnd

Work next rnd very loosely.
Rnd 9: Place bead to back of each st and make 1dc in each st, sl st into last st.
Fasten off yarn.
Turn cosy with beads on the outside.

Abbreviations (see page 19)

ch chain

dc double crochet

dc2tog double crochet 2 together

rep repeat

rnd round

sl st slip stitch

st(s) stitch(es)

Techniques (see pages 10–19)

Fastening off

Joining in a new colour

Starting to work in the round

3 ### Finishing the cosy

Weave in the yarn ends with the darning needle. Cut a piece of ribbon 6cm (2½in) long. Hem the two ends to prevent fraying and sew the ends together to make a tab. Sew the tab onto the top of each cosy using small stitches hidden inside the crochet.

Sweets

These fun-to-make sweets use metallic and bright yarns to represent the shiny and colourful wrappers. Have fun and make your own sweet shop!

You will need

Yarn A: 1 x 100g ball (280m/306yd) DMC Petra no 3 (100% long staple cotton), in each of:

shade 5742, yellow

shade 53845, blue

shade 5907, green

shade 53805, pink

Yarn B: 1 x 20g ball (150m/164yd) DMC Metallic Crochet Thread (60% viscose, 40% metallized polyester), in each of:

shade L677, gold

shade L796, blue

3.25mm crochet hook

Stitch marker

Darning needle

Toy stuffing

Measurements

One size, each sweet is approx 10cm (4in) long

Tension

Exact tension isn't important for this project but make sure that you crochet tightly so that the stuffing does not show.

1 Crochet the sweet

Using 3.25mm hook and any yarn A, ch20, join into a ring with a sl st into first ch.

Rnd 1: Ch1, 1dc in each st to end of rnd.

Rnd 2: 1dc in each st around.

Rep last row until sweet measures approx 8cm (3in) long.

Fasten off yarn.

Join any yarn B to one open edge of sweet.

Next rnd: Ch1, miss 1 dc, 5tr in next st, *miss 1 dc, 1dc in next st, miss 1 dc, 5tr in next st, rep from * to last st, miss last dc, sl st into first ch to join rnd.

Repeat the last round at the opposite end of the sweet.

2 Gather the end

Use a darning needle to weave in all ends. Use a needle to thread a piece of yarn in and out of the stitches all round one end of the sweet, approx 2.5cm (1in) in from the end. Pull up the thread tightly to draw in the end of the sweet wrapper and fasten off securely.

Make your own pick 'n' mix!

Abbreviations (see page 19)

ch chain

dc double crochet

rep repeat

rnd round

Techniques (see pages 10–19)

Fastening off

Joining in a new colour

Marking rounds with a stitch marker

Starting to work in the round

NOTE Sweets are worked in a continuous spiral, do not turn throughout and do not join rounds.

③ Finish the sweet

Stuff the sweet with small tufts of toy stuffing until it is nice and round. Use the end of a pencil or the blunt end of a crochet hook to push the stuffing in well. Sew round the opposite, open end of the sweet in the same way as the first end, approx 2.5cm (1in) in from the end. Make lots of sweets in different colours for a tempting treat!

Crochet cakes

These little cakes look so sweet you'll find it hard to believe you can't really eat them. You can make just one type or all three for a teatime treat for your dolls.

You will need

1 x 50g ball (125m/137yd) Millamia Merino (100% merino wool), in each of:

Yarn A: shade 160, fawn

Yarn B: shade 122, petal

Yarn C: shade 104, claret

Yarn D: shade 124, snow

3.25mm crochet hook

Stitch marker

Darning needle

Toy stuffing

Sewing needle and thread

Beads and buttons for decoration

Measurements

Cupcake: approx 10cm (4in) diameter

Doughnut: approx 12cm (4¾in) diameter

Sponge cake: approx 6cm (2½in) diameter and 9cm (3½in) tall

Tension

Exact tension isn't important for this project but make sure that you crochet tightly so that the stuffing does not show.

Crochet the cupcake

Using 3.25mm hook and yarn A, ch2.

Rnd 1: 6dc in first ch, join into a ring with a sl st.

Rnd 2: 2dc in each st around join with a sl st into top of first st. (12 dc)

Rnd 3: [1dc, 2dc in next st] around. (18 dc)

Rnd 4: [2dc, 2dc in next st] around. (24 dc)

Rnd 5: [3dc, 2dc in next st] around. (30 dc)

Rnd 6: [4dc, 2dc in next st] around. (36 dc)

Rnd 7: [5dc, 2dc in next st] around. (42 dc)

Rnd 8: [6dc, 2dc in next st] around, join with a sl st into top of first st. (48 dc)

Work 1 rnd straight in dc (blo), join with a sl st into top of first st.

Work straight in dc for 7 more rnds, in spirals, do not join rnds.

Next rnd: *Ch3, sl st (tfl) of next st; rep from * all round, join rnd with a sl st.

Fasten off yarn A.

Join yarn B to the unworked back loop in any st of last dc rnd.

Next rnd: 1dc (blo) in each unworked back loop of last dc rnd, join rnd with a sl st.

Work 4 rnds straight in dc in spirals, do not join rounds.

Next rnd: [6dc, dc2tog] around, join rnd with a sl st. (42 dc)

Work 1 rnd straight without shaping.

Next rnd: [5dc, dc2tog] around, join rnd with a sl st. (36 dc)

Work 1 rnd straight without shaping.

Next rnd: [4dc, dc2tog] around, join rnd with a sl st. (30 dc)

Work 1 rnd straight without shaping.

With the yarn and hook still attached, stuff the cake through the hole until it is firm and nicely shaped.

Next rnd: [3dc, dc2tog] around, join rnd with a sl st. (24 dc)

Next rnd: [2dc, dc2tog] around, join rnd with a sl st. (18 dc)

Next rnd: [1dc, dc2tog] around, join rnd with a sl st. (12 dc)

Next rnd: [Dc2tog] around, join rnd with a sl st. (6 dc)

Sew round the remaining hole and pull up to secure.

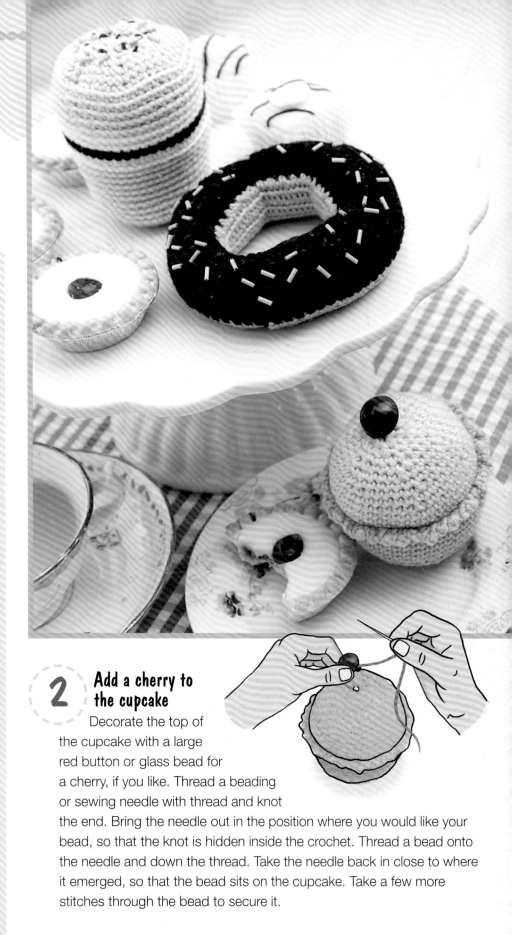

Abbreviations (see page 19)

blo back loop only

ch chain

dc double crochet

dc2tog double crochet 2 together

rep repeat

rnd round

tfl through front loop

Techniques (see pages 10–19)

Fastening off

Joining in a new colour

Marking rounds with a stitch marker

Starting to work in the round

NOTE Pieces are worked in a continuous spiral, do not turn throughout and do not join rounds unless otherwise stated.

2 Add a cherry to the cupcake

Decorate the top of the cupcake with a large red button or glass bead for a cherry, if you like. Thread a beading or sewing needle with thread and knot the end. Bring the needle out in the position where you would like your bead, so that the knot is hidden inside the crochet. Thread a bead onto the needle and down the thread. Take the needle back in close to where it emerged, so that the bead sits on the cupcake. Take a few more stitches through the bead to secure it.

3 Crochet the sponge cake

Using 3.25mm hook and yarn B, ch2.

Rnd 1: 6dc in first ch.

Rnd 2: 2dc in each st around join with a sl st into top of first st. (12 dc)

Rnd 3: [1dc, 2dc in next st] around. (18 dc)

Rnd 4: [2dc, 2dc in next st] around. (24 dc)

Rnd 5: [3dc, 2dc in next st] around. (30 dc)

Rnd 6: [4dc, 2dc in next st] around. (36 dc)

Rnd 7: [5dc, 2dc in next st] around. (42 dc)

Rnd 8: [6dc, 2dc in next st] around. (48 dc)

Work 1 rnd straight in dc (blo).

Work straight in dc (blo) for 7 more rnds.

4 Add sprinkles

Sew sprinkles on top of the cake either using a few single stitches of contrasting yarn or attach bugle beads, as for the cherry in step 2.

Change to yarn D and work straight in dc (blo) for 2 more rnds.

Change to yarn C and work 1 rnd straight in dc.

Change to yarn D and work straight in dc (blo) for 2 more rnds.

Change to yarn B and work straight in dc (blo) for 5 more rnds.

Next rnd: *6dc (blo), dc2tog (blo); rep from * around. (42 dc)

Begin to stuff cake to desired fullness.

Next rnd: [5dc, dc2tog] around. (36 dc)

Next rnd: [4dc, dc2tog] around. (30 dc)

Next rnd: [3dc, dc2tog] around. (24 dc)

Next rnd: [2dc, dc2tog] around. (18 dc)

Next rnd: [1dc, dc2tog] around. (12 dc)

Next rnd: [Dc2tog] around. (6 dc)

Fasten off yarn.

Sew round the remaining hole and pull up to secure.

5 Crochet the doughnut

Using 3.25mm hook and yarn A, ch65, join into ring with a sl st into first ch, being careful not to twist the chain.

Rnd 1: Ch1, 1dc in each ch to end of rnd, join to first ch with a sl st.

Rnd 2: Ch1, 1dc (blo) in each st to end of rnd, join to first ch with a sl st.

Work last rnd 5 times more.

Change to yarn C.

Next rnd: Ch1, 1dc in each st to end of rnd, join to first ch with a sl st.

Work last rnd 9 times more.

Fasten off yarn leaving a long tail.

6 Sew together

Fold the top and bottom edges so that they meet and form a doughnut shape. Thread the yarn tail onto a darning needle and sew the edges together with whip stitch, without twisting, leaving a gap for stuffing.

Good enough to eat!

7 Finish the doughnut

Stuff the doughnut with toy stuffing through the gap until it is firm and nicely shaped. Sew up the remaining seam. You can decorate the top of the doughnut with colourful bugle beads as in step 4, or sew sprinkles on top of the cake using a few single stitches of contrasting yarn.

Cafetière cosy

A fun and easy project that makes a great gift for coffee lovers. It will keep the coffee in the pot toastie and warm. The colours are changed at random as you work, for a multi-colour effect.

You will need

1 x 50g ball (94m/103yd) Rooster Almerino Aran (50% baby alpaca, 50% merino wool), in each of:

shade 305, custard

shade 310, rooster

shade 307, Brighton rock

shade 309, ocean

shade 302, sugared almond

shade 303, strawberry cream

shade 308, spiced plum

5mm crochet hook

Darning needle

1 small button

Measurements

To fit a medium-size 4–6 cup cafetière, approx 31cm (12in) circumference

Tension

16dc x 20 rows over 10cm (4in) square, using 5mm hook or size to obtain correct tension.

1 Crochet the cosy

Using 5mm crochet hook and any colour, ch46.

Row 1: 1dc in next ch from hook, 1dc in each ch to end, turn. (45 sts)

Row 2: Ch1, 1dc in each st to end, turn.

Rep Row 2, changing colours randomly every 2, 3 or 4 rows, until work measures 16cm (6¼in), or to just above handle of cafetière. Do not fasten off.

2 Make the buttonhole and button tab

Ch5, 1dc in next ch from hook, 1dc in each st to end.

Next row: 1dc in each st to last 4 sts, ch2, miss 2 sts, 1dc in each of next 2 sts.

Next row: Ch1, 1dc in each of next 2 sts, 2dc in next ch sp, 1dc in each st to end.

Next row: 1dc in each st to end. Do not fasten off.

Work dc around button tab by making 2dc around side, 1dc in each of the sts underneath to end. Make sl st into straight edge. Fasten off yarn.

3 Finish the cosy

With the wrong side facing you, join the two short edges by sewing them together for 2.5cm (1in) up from the bottom, leaving the remainder open, using a matching yarn.

Abbreviations (see page 19)

ch chain

dc double crochet

rep repeat

sl st slip stitch

st(s) stitch(es)

Techniques (see pages 10–19)

Fastening off

Joining in a new colour

Sewing on buttons

Turn

4 Sew the button

Turn right side out. Sew a button on the opposite side to the buttonhole tab to correspond with the buttonhole. Weave in the loose ends with a darning needle.

Keep the coffee steaming hot!

Jam pot covers

These fun jam pot covers are really quick and perfect for beginners. You can use any yarn — just choose two pretty colours for the perfect finish for a jar of homemade jam. These would make great thank-you gifts for your teacher!

1 Crochet the cover
Both sizes

Using 4mm hook and yarn A, ch2, 6dc in second ch from hook, join into a ring with a sl st.

Rnd 1: Ch3 (counts as first tr), make 1tr in same st as 3ch, 2tr in next and each st to end, join with a sl st into top of first 3-ch. (12 sts)

Rnd 2: Ch3, make 1tr in same st as 3ch, 2tr in next and each st to end, join with a sl st into top of first 3-ch. (24 sts)

Rnd 3: Ch3, make 2tr in each of next 2 sts; *1tr in next st, 2tr in each of next 2 sts; rep from * to end, join with a sl st into top of first 3-ch. (40 sts)

Rnd 4: Ch3, make 1tr in each of next 2 sts, *2tr in next st, 1tr in each of next 3 sts; rep from * to last st, 2tr, join with a sl st into top of first 3-ch. (50 sts)

Rnd 5: Ch3, make 1tr in next st, *2tr in next st, 1tr in each of next 2 sts; rep from * to last st, 1tr, join with a sl st into top of first 3-ch. (66 sts)

For large size only

Rnd 6: Ch3, make 1tr in each st, join with a sl st into top of first 3-ch. (66 sts)

Fasten off yarn A and join yarn B.

Rnd 7: With the right side facing you, miss 1 st *5tr in next st, miss 1 st, sl st; rep from * to last st, sl st. Fasten off yarn.

You will need

Colourway 1 (light pink)

1 x 50g ball (112.5m/124yd) Rooster Almerino DK (50% baby alpaca, 50% merino wool) in each of:

shade 203, strawberry cream (A)

shade 201, cornish (B)

Colourway 2 (lavender)

1 x 50g ball (90m/98yd) Debbie Bliss Cashmerino Aran (55% merino wool, 33% microfibre, 12% cashmere) in shade 019, lilac (A)

1 x 50g ball (112.5m/124yd) Rooster Almerino DK (50% baby alpaca, 50% merino wool) in shade 207, gooseberry (B)

Colourway 3 (green)

1 x 50g ball (85m/93yd) Rowan Handknit Cotton DK (100% cotton) in shade 219, gooseberry (A)

1 x 50g ball (112.5m/124yd) Rooster Almerino DK (50% baby alpaca, 50% merino wool) in shade 211, Brighton rock (B)

Colourway 4 (bright pink)

1 x 50g ball (112.5m/124yd) Rooster Almerino DK (50% baby alpaca, 50% merino wool) in each of:

shade 211, Brighton rock (A)

shade 201, cornish (B)

4mm crochet hook

Elastic band

Approx 40cm (16in) trim or braiding in a contrasting colour

Measurements

Standard: 15cm (6in) diameter

Large: 18cm (7in) diameter

Tension

Exact tension isn't important for this project.

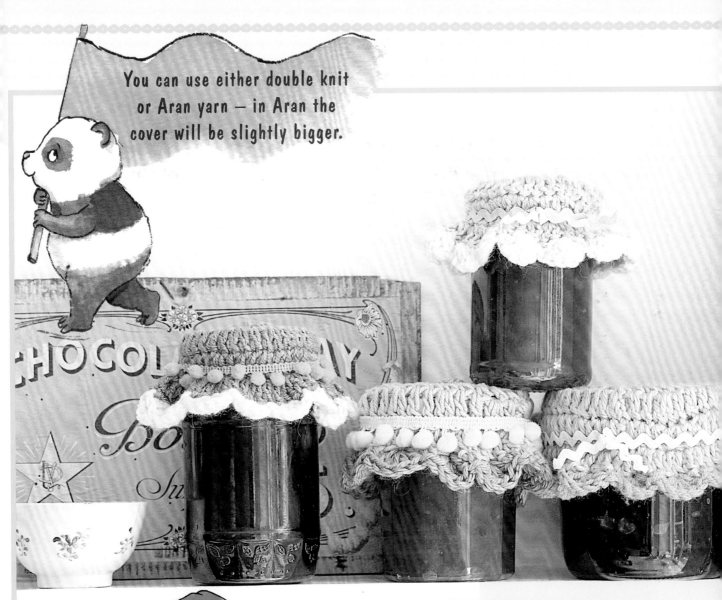

You can use either double knit or Aran yarn — in Aran the cover will be slightly bigger.

Finish the cover

2 Place the cover on top of the jar lid and secure with an elastic band. Finish off by tying the trim or braiding around the top, knotting to secure it in place.

Make pretty pots for a sweet treat

Abbreviations (see page 19)

ch chain

dc double crochet

dc2tog double crochet 2 together

rnd round

sl st slip stitch

st(s) stitch(es)

tr treble

Techniques (see pages 10–19)

Fastening off

Joining in a new colour

Starting to work in the round

Mushroom

This fun mushroom is great for decorating your room and would look super cute on your bed sitting alongside Cheryl the snail on page 100 and the little penguin on page 122.

You will need

1 x 50g ball (75m/81yd) Sirdar Click Chunky with wool (70% acrylic, 30% wool) in each of:

Yarn A: shade 142, lamb

Yarn B: shade 163, really red

5mm crochet hook

Stitch marker

Darning needle

Toy stuffing

Buttons for decoration

Sewing needle and thread

Scraps of yarn for embroidery

Measurements

Approx 10cm (4in) high

Tension

Exact tension isn't important for this project but make sure that you crochet tightly so that the stuffing does not show.

(1) Crochet the mushroom stalk

Using 5mm hook and yarn A, ch2.

Rnd 1: 6dc in first ch made, do not join rnd.

Rnd 2: 2dc in each dc around. (12 dc)

Rnd 3: [2dc in next st, 1dc] around. (18 dc)

Rnd 4: [2dc in next st, 2dc] around. (24 dc)

Rnd 5: [2dc in next st, 3dc] around. (30 dc)

Work 1 rnd straight in dc (blo), join with a sl st into top of first st.

Work straight in dc for 5 more rnds, in spirals, do not join rnds.

Next rnd: [3dc, dc2tog] around. (24 dc)

Work 1 row straight in dc.

Next rnd: [2dc, dc2tog] around. (18 dc)

Fasten off yarn A, join in yarn B.

Stuff the stalk before crocheting the cap.

Cute as a button!

Abbreviations (see page 19)

blo back loop only

ch chain

dc double crochet

dc2tog double crochet 2 stitches together

rep repeat

rnd round

sl st slip stitch

st(s) stitch(es)

Techniques (see pages 10–19)

Fastening off

Joining in a new colour

Marking rounds with a stitch marker

Sewing on buttons

Starting to work in the round

NOTE The mushroom is worked in a continuous spiral, do not turn throughout and do not join rounds.

2 Crochet the mushroom cap

Work 1 row straight in dc.
Next rnd: 2dc in each dc around.
(36 dc)
Next rnd: [2dc in next st, 1dc] around.
(54 dc)
Work 3 rows straight in dc (blo).
Begin to decrease as follows:
Rnd 1: [4dc, dc2tog] around. (45 dc)
Work 1 row straight in dc. Begin to
stuff cap.
Rnd 3: [3dc, dc2tog] around. (36 dc)
Rnd 4: [2dc, dc2tog] around. (27 dc)
Rnd 5: [1dc, dc2tog] around. (18 dc)
Dc2tog around until hole closed.
Fasten off yarn and stitch remaining
hole closed.

3 Decorate the cap

Using a sewing needle and
thread, sew a few buttons to
the cap for spots.

4 Add a face

Using a darning needle and
some leftover yarn in a dark
colour, embroider a simple face on
the stalk of the mushroom. Use a
few straight stitches grouped
together for the eyes, and add a
smiley mouth in backstitch.

If you're making this as a gift for a baby, replace the buttons with circles of felt.

Juggling balls

Crocheted balls are fabulous for playing games such as Piggy in the Middle or Hacky Sack, and are perfect for learning to juggle. To give them some weight when juggling, fill with beans or PVC beanbag granules.

You will need

1 x 100g ball (400m/437yd) DMC Petra no 5 (100% long staple cotton), in each of:

Yarn A: shade 5742, yellow

Yarn B: shade 54230, blue

Yarn C: shade 5907, green

2.25mm crochet hook

PVC beanbag beans

Darning needle

Measurements

One size, approx 6cm (2½in) diameter

Tension

Exact tension isn't important for this project, but make sure that you crochet tightly so that the beans do not show through the stitches.

1 Crochet the ball

Using 2.25mm crochet hook and any colour yarn, ch2.

Rnd 1: 6dc in first ch made, join with a sl st into top of first st.

Rnd 2: Ch1, 2dc in each dc to end, join with a sl st into 1-ch. (12 dc)

Rnd 3: Ch1, [2dc in next st, 1dc] to end, join with a sl st into 1-ch. (18 dc)

Rnd 4: Ch1, [2dc in next st, 2dc] to end, join with a sl st into 1-ch. (24 dc)

Rnd 5: Ch1, [2dc in next st, 3dc] to end, join with a sl st into 1-ch. (30 dc)

Work 1 rnd straight in dc without increasing.

Rnd 7: Ch1, [2dc in next st, 4dc] to end, join with a sl st into 1-ch. (36 dc)

Work 1 rnd straight in dc without increasing.

Rnd 8: Ch1, [2dc in next st, 5dc] to end, join with a sl st into 1-ch. (42 dc)

Work 1 rnd straight in dc without increasing.

Rnd 9: Ch1, [2dc in next st, 6dc] to end, join with a sl st into 1-ch. (48 dc)

Work 9 rnds straight in dc without increasing.

Begin to decrease as follows:

Rnd 19: Ch1, [dc2tog, 6dc] to end, join with a sl st into 1-ch. (42 dc)

Work 1 rnd straight in dc without decreasing.

Rnd 21: Ch1, [dc2tog, 5dc] to end, join with a sl st into 1-ch. (36 dc)

Work 1 rnd straight in dc without decreasing.

Rnd 23: Ch1, [dc2tog, 4dc] to end, join with a sl st into 1-ch. (30 dc)

Work 1 rnd straight in dc without decreasing. Begin stuffing the ball with beanbag beans through the hole until firm.

Rnd 25: Ch1, [dc2tog, 3dc] to end, join with a sl st into 1-ch. (24 dc)

Rnd 26: Ch1, [dc2tog, 2dc] to end, join with a sl st into 1-ch. (18 dc)

Rnd 27: Ch1, [dc2tog, 1dc] to end, join with a sl st into 1-ch. (12 dc)

Rnd 28: Dc2tog evenly all round. (6 dc)

Fasten off yarn.

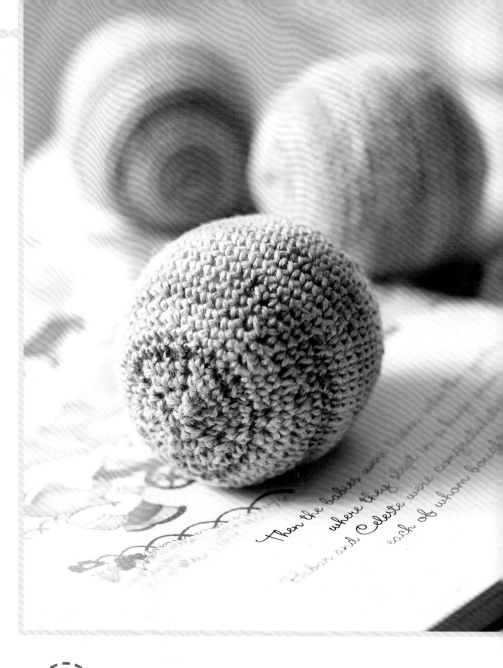

Abbreviations (see page 19)

ch chain

dc double crochet

dc2tog double crochet 2 together

rnd round

sl st slip stitch

Techniques (see pages 10–19)

Fastening off

Joining in a new colour

Making fabric

Starting to work in the round

NOTE The balls are worked in complete rounds.

Begin stuffing each ball from rnd 24 to ensure an evenly filled ball.

Work 2 rows of each colour alternately, or in any order you like.

2 ### Finish the ball

Add some more beanbag beans through the hole in the top until the ball is nearly full, then thread the fastened-off yarn onto a darning needle and sew up the hole to close it.

Penguin

This perky penguin is just calling to have his tummy squished! Why not try making him a scarf to keep him warm at the South Pole?

You will need

1 x 50g ball (125m/137yd) Millamia Merino (100% merino wool), in each of:

Yarn A: shade 101, midnight navy

Yarn B: shade 142, daisy yellow

Yarn C: shade 124, snow white

3.25mm crochet hook

Stitch marker

Darning needle

Toy stuffing

Buttons for eyes

Sewing needle and thread

Measurements

One size, approx 14cm (5½in) tall

Tension

Exact tension isn't important for this project but make sure that you crochet tightly so that the stuffing does not show.

1 ### Crochet the head and body

Using 3.25mm crochet hook and yarn A, ch2.

Rnd 1: 7dc in first ch made, do not join rnd.

Rnd 2: 2dc in each dc around. (14 dc)

Rnd 3: [2dc in next st, 1dc] around. (21 dc)

Rnd 4: [2dc in next st, 2dc] around. (28 dc)

Rnd 5: [2dc in next st, 3dc] around. (35 dc)

Work 5 rnds straight in dc without increasing.

Begin to decrease as follows:

Rnd 11: [Dc2tog, 3dc] around. (28 dc)

Rnd 12: [Dc2tog, 2dc] around. (21 dc)

Stuff head fully.

Work 2 rnds straight in dc without decreasing.

Rnd 15: [2dc in next st, 2dc] around. (28 dc)

Rnd 16: [2dc in next st, 3dc] around. (35 dc)

Rnd 17: [2dc in next st, 4dc] around. (42 dc)

Work 1 rnd straight in dc without increasing.

Rnd 19: [2dc in next st, 5dc] around. (49 dc)

Work 1 rnd straight in dc without increasing.

Rnd 21: [2dc in next st, 6dc] around. (56 dc)

Work 1 rnd straight in dc without increasing.

Rnd 22: [2dc in next st, 7dc] around. (63 dc)

Work 3 rnds straight in dc without increasing.

Begin to decrease, as follows:

Rnd 26: [Dc2tog, 7dc] around. (56 dc)

Work 1 rnd straight in dc without decreasing.

Rnd 28: [Dc2tog, 6dc] around. (49 dc)

Work 1 rnd straight in dc without decreasing.

Rnd 30: [Dc2tog, 5dc] around. (42 dc)

Give your penguin a name

Work 1 rnd straight in dc without decreasing. With the hook still attached, begin to stuff the body through the hole.

Rnd 32: [Dc2tog, 4dc] around. (35 dc)

Rnd 33: [Dc2tog, 3dc] around. (28 dc)

Rnd 34: [Dc2tog, 2dc] around. (21 dc)

Rnd 35: [Dc2tog, 1dc] around. (14 dc)

Rnd 36: [Dc2tog] around. (7 dc)
Fasten off yarn and sew up the hole in the top of the head to secure.

Abbreviations (see page 19)

ch chain
dc double crochet
dc2tog double crochet 2 together
rnd round

Techniques (see pages 10–19)

Fastening off

Sewing on buttons

Marking rounds with a stitch marker

Starting to work in the round

NOTE The wings and feet are worked in rows, turn at the end of each row.

The body and beak are worked in continuous spiral rounds, do not turn throughout and do not join rounds.

2 Crochet the feet (make two)

Using 3.25mm crochet hook and yarn B, ch4.

Row 1: 1dc in 2nd ch from hook, 1dc in each ch to end, turn. (3 dc)

Row 2: Ch1, 2dc in first st, 1dc, 2dc in last st, turn. (5 dc)

Row 3: Ch1, 1dc to end of row, turn.

Row 4: Ch1, 2dc in first st, 1dc, 2dc in last st, turn. (7 dc)

Row 5: Ch1, 1dc to end of row.

Fasten off yarn.

3 Crochet the wings (make two)

Using 3.25mm crochet hook and yarn A, ch3.

Row 1: 1dc in 2nd ch from hook, 1dc in next chain, turn. (2 dc)

Row 2: Ch1, 2dc in first st, 2dc in last st, turn. (4 dc)

Row 3: Ch1, 2dc in first st, 2dc, 2dc in last st, turn. (6 dc)

Rows 4–6: Ch1, 1dc to end of row, turn.

Fasten off yarn.

4 Crochet the beak

Using 3.25mm crochet hook and yarn B, ch3. Work in the round in spirals.

Rnd 1: 5dc in 2nd ch from hook, do not turn.

Work 1 rnd straight.

Rnd 3: 2dc in each dc around. (10 dc)

Fasten off yarn.

5 Crochet the tummy

Using 3.25mm crochet hook and yarn C, ch2.

Work in the round in spirals.

Rnd 1: 6dc in 2nd ch from hook, do not turn.

Rnd 2: 2dc in each dc around. (12 dc)

Rnd 3: [1dc, 2dc in next st] around. (18 dc)

Rnd 4: 3dc, 3tr, 6dc, 3tr, 1dc to end of rnd, join with a sl st to top of first dc.

Fasten off yarn.

6 Sew on the wings and feet

Using a darning needle, sew the wings to the sides of the body and the feet to the bottom of the body. You can use the yarn end to attach the pieces with whip stitch.

7 Sew on the tummy and beak

Using a darning needle and whip stitch, sew the white oval to the penguin's tummy. Then sew the beak to the middle of the head.

8 Sew on the eyes

Finally, sew on buttons for the eyes, hiding the end of the thread in the crochet.

Suppliers and Resources

The yarns used in these projects should be available from your local yarn or craft store. If you can't find the correct yarn, then try the websites listed here.

YARN SUPPLIERS

Blue Faced Yarn Shop
H W Hammand & Co
The Croft Stables
Station Lane
Great Barrow
Cheshire
CH3 7JN
www.bluefaced.com

Dancing Hens Craft Studio
Wool, books and tuition
Battlers Green Farm
Radlett
Hertfordshire
WD7 8PH
01923 856619
www.dancinghens.com

Debbie Bliss Yarns
Designer Yarns
Units 8-10
Newbridge Industrial Estate
Pitt Street
Keighley
West Yorkshire
BD21 4PQ
01535 664222
www.designeryarns.uk.com

Fyberspates
The Maintenance Room
The Nalder Estate
East Challow
Nr Wantage
Oxfordshire
OX12 9SY
07540 656660
www.fyberspates.co.uk

Ingrid Wagner
Giant crochet supplies
Studio 5
The Stone Barn
Kirkharle Courtyard
Kirkharle
Northumberland
NE19 2PE
01830 540117
www.ingridwagner.com

John Lewis
Stores nationwide
0845 604 9049
www.johnlewis.com

Natural Dye Studio
Moors Farm
Hollesley
Woodbridge
Suffolk
IP12 3RF
01394 411500
www.thenaturaldyestudio.com

Rooster Yarns
Laughing Hens online
Wool, patterns, knitting & crochet supplies
www.laughinghens.com
01829 740903

Rowan Yarns
Green Lane Mill
Holmfirth
West Yorkshire
HD9 2DX
01484 681881
www.knitrowan.com

VV Rouleaux
Ribbons and trimmings
101 Marylebone Lane
London W1U 2QD
020 7224 5179
www.vvrouleaux.com

TUITION
Nicki Trench Workshops
Crochet, knitting, and craft workshops,
all levels
Email: nicki@nickitrench.com

Index

rows, working in 16

S

sausage dog draught excluder 90–2
scarves
    skinny scarf 26
    squares scarf 40–1
scissors 8
sewing needle and thread 8
sewing up 18
skinny scarf 26
slip knot 10
slip stitch 12
squares scarf 40–1
stitch marker 8, 16
stitches 11–15
storage jars 82–3
suppliers 126–7
sweets 106–7

T

techniques 10–18
tools and materials 8
toys
    baby bouncers 98–9
    Cheryl the snail 100–3
    crochet cakes 108–11
    juggling balls 120–1
    mushroom 116–19
    enguin 122–5
    sweets 106–7
treble (tr) 13
triple treble (trtr) 14
turn 16

W

whip stitch 18
working in the round 15–16
working into a chain space 16
working into back loop (blo) 16
working into front loop (tfl) 16
working straight 16

Y

yarn round hook 11
yarns 8
    cutting 8
    holding 11
    joining in new yarn 17
    suppliers 126–7
    weaving in yarn ends 17

Z

zigzag bolster 84–5

Acknowledgments

Key: t = top, c = center, b = bottom, l = left, r = right

Project makers
Catherine Hirst: pp 58, 86

Claire Montgomerie: pp 22, 24, 26, 34, 36, 40, 42, 44, 48, 60, 62, 66, 68, 74, 82, 84, 90, 93, 106, 108, 116, 120, 122

Nicki Trench: pp 30, 52, 70, 78, 88, 98, 100, 104, 112, 114

Photography
Emma Mitchell: pp 2, 3l, 3r, 8t, 19, 31, 33, 53, 55, 56l, 56c, 58, 59, 71, 73, 76, 77l, 77c, 78, 79, 81, 87, 88, 89, 97l, 97c, 98, 99, 101, 112, 113, 115

Martin Norris: pp 3c, 4, 5t, 5b, 6, 7, 8b, 9, 12, 15, 17, 18, 20, 21, 23, 25, 27, 29, 35, 37, 39, 41, 43, 45, 47, 49, 50, 51, 56, 57r, 61, 63, 65, 67, 68, 69, 75, 77r, 83, 85, 91, 92, 93, 95, 96, 97r, 102, 103, 105, 107, 109, 110, 111, 117, 119, 121, 123, 124